# Fulfilling Your Destiny With Ease

A divine map to satisfaction in life

by
Harrison I. Enudi

For further information, contact:
DESTINY AWARENESS OUTREACH, SOUTH KOREA.
E-mail: dao@pastorharrisonenudi.org, contact@pastorharrisonenudi.org
Web: www.pastorharrisonenudi.org

ISBN: 978-1-4669-1952-5 (sc)
ISBN: 978-1-4669-1951-8 (e)

All scriptures quotations are from the king James Version of the Bible, except otherwise stated.

*Our mission is to efficiently provide the world's finest, most comprehensive book publishing service, enabling every author to experience success. To find out how to publish your book, your way, and have it available worldwide, visit us online at www.trafford.com*

*Trafford rev. 05/15/12*

 www.trafford.com

**North America & international**
toll-free: 1 888 232 4444 (USA & Canada)
phone: 250 383 6864 ♦ fax:812 355 4082

# CONTENTS

# FOREWORD

IT IS JOB, THE patriarch, who requested God; in the middle of an overwhelming crisis, saying, "Teach me what I cannot see" (Job 34:32 N.I.V). We need to also draw toward God for what we do not know, what we cannot discover about ourselves, our destinies, potentials and purposes for being on earth.

The patriarch sure must have attended some secular system of education in his days in order to acquire education that would position him to make a success of his life. But it was not until his epic encounter with God that the extent of his ignorance dawned on him. And he begged God to teach him what he could not see—destiny fulfillment.

This book's phenomenon tells volumes about whole crowds of educated, intelligent, wealthy and famous people steeped in ignorance about themselves and their destinies, which they are yet to "fulfill with ease". The phenomenon equally exposes the faults in our educational system which has little or no room for the spiritual or God; and it tells about our warped concepts of life and how we ought to live it, seeing they are not to the praise of God, but to the satisfaction of ourselves, friends, relations, teachers and even some maverick pastors.

It is this dangerous flaw that is the root of much of the chaos in destiny discovery in our individual, family, community and national lives. For when we don't discover where we ought to be or what we ought do in life at any given time (even if it is through trial and error), most of us will be in the wrong place and doing the wrong thing not because we have found destiny or problems to solve for others, but merely to survive; and in beginning to try to survive without beginning to fulfill our destiny, we perish half way.

It is at this juncture that there is need for us to pause, reflect, look for new direction based on revealed teachings from God through whatever means it has pleased God to transmit information to us. Inspired books are usually the most common means through which God reaches out to people in distress, pain and agony and confusion about their destinies. ". . . I, Daniel, understood by books the number of the years; where of the word of the Lord came to Jeremiah, which he would accomplish . . ." (Daniel 9:2). Then Daniel went on to discover and fulfill his destiny.

In this book, "Fulfilling Your Destiny With Ease", author Harrison I. Enudi serves us a well-written and deep book that tells us what we ought to know and do to fulfill our destinies in line with God's will. This excellent book will not have you as it found you, if only you take time to digest and not merely read its pruning and incisive content; for it unclothes us for spiritual and moral circumcision. It lays bare the futility made of our lives by pursuing the wrong ambition, accumulation of wealth, self promotion, mistaken location of purpose and place (or geography), etc. which leave us unfulfilled, empty and disappointed with life, one another, and even with God.

The content of this book strikes us with awe and forces a sobering attitude down our throats. It is gently bitter in a very constructive way like those bitter syrups you give to infants; in the end you recover your mental balance, spiritual direction and moral health, and set again for a sure journey with God in the fulfillment of your destiny.

Therefore, we highly and whole-heartedly recommend this inspirational, motivational and devotional piece to all and sundry that is in search of his or her destiny with an unquenchable passion to be fulfilled in every area of life.

Editorial team,

High Calling Outreach Publishers,

Port Harcourt,

Nigeria

# ACKNOWLEDGEMENTS

WHEN GOD GAVE ME this commission, I mean, when he revealed the purpose of my life to me, I was ignorant about how to carry it out. I had but a little knowledge of what **'destiny'** is. It was through books I got to understand that to every mission given to anyone divinely, there is a mentor or mentors who are bridges to the future of protégés.

I want to appreciate the great men of God, whose books have really affected my life and ministry, like Dr. David O Oyedepo, Dr. Mike Murdock, Dr. Myles Munroe, Dr. K. C. Treat, Pastor W. F. Kumuyi, Dr. David (Paul) Yonggi Cho, Kenneth E. Hagin and many others.

I would like also to appreciate the ministers in whose hands God brought me up, especially Pastor Mike Enebeli (late) and Pastor Kennedy Annieh, from my hometown. May the Almighty God bless them for me!

Let me not also forget the instruments that God used to make sure that this book is in the streets of the universe today: Ambassador Desmond Akawor from Nigeria, Pastor Vernon Johnson from the United State of America and My father in the Lord, Rev. Moses Mckonteh from Sierra Leone; by whose hands, God lifted me to where I am today. May God continue to increase His grace on their lives in Jesus name!

# DEDICATION

I HEREBY DEDICATE THIS life-changing book to God Almighty. I thank God for the success of its authorship. I, convincingly, believe it will bless the lives of people as they read with care, this unusual revelations from heaven; and as they discover and apply the secrets in it, may the Lord cause an unusual turn-around in their lives in Jesus precious name! Amen.

# INTRODUCTION

ARE YOU SO CONFUSED in life that you don't know what to do, where to go from where you are, or how to pursue your life in a fruitful and positive direction? Do you feel inferior before others, believing you are a nonentity? Are you an apprentice and you are not happy about your choice of skill acquisition? Are you in any institution studying one of the courses and you are not satisfied with it? Are you in business and it is static or experiencing 'ups' and 'downs'? Are you working in any of company and you are not fulfilled? Are you a civil servant and have no joy doing your job? Have you ever one day sat down to reason out what you are really born to do as regards to your destiny? Do you have fulfillment in life involving in that work? Do you have peace of mind? Do you not feel you have left something somewhere in your life? Have you found out your importance to your generation? Are you confused about who should be your spouse?

Without locating an answer to any of the above questions that perhaps applies to you, you may not really matter to anyone on earth. Your life is expected to be a solution to a particular problem in the lives of people. Until you find God's will and purpose for your life, you will never be fulfilled; and without that, your true life is not yet begun.

Now, how can you find an answer to any of the above questions that may be applying to you?

*"They know not, neither will they understand; they walk on in darkness: all the foundations of the earth are out of course"* (Psalm 82:5)

But God has a favor for your life. Hear his promise: *"And I will give you pastors according to my heart, which shall feed you with knowledge and understanding"* (Jeremiah 3:15)

This is why God has sent me your way now. This book is written out of a burden to put your feet on your purposed track of life and to terminate your frustration, confusion and stagnation. I am a messenger sent by God, by his power and wisdom, to repair the desolations of many generations; to enlighten the eyes of people's understanding to know their different callings and the glory of the latent potentials within them, to awaken generations from slumber, to restore men back to their garden of Eden, to remove the barriers to progression in people's businesses prophetically; and to rearrange the scattered ministries and destinies of men by the Spirit of God, and by his word.

Your predicaments and failures could be traceable to your ignorance towards your potentials, your worth and your make-up. It could be traceable to your inability to transmute your dream or vision into its physical equivalence.

*"My people are destroyed for lack of knowledge . . ."* (Hosea 4:6)

*"Now will I sing to my well beloved touching his vineyard: My well beloved hath a vine yard in a very fruitful hill: And he fenced it, and gathered out the stones thereof, and planted it with the choicest vine, and built a tower in the midst of it, and also made a wine press therein: and he looked that it should bring forth grapes, and it brought forth wild grapes. And now, inhabitants of Jerusalem, and men of Judah, Judge, I pray you, betwixt me and my vineyard. What could have been done more to my vineyard that I have not done in it? Wherefore, when it looked that is should bring forth grapes, brought it forth wild grapes?"* (Isaiah 5:1-4)

By the above scriptures, you can see that you are heavily loaded as God's choicest vine, and planted in a very fruitful hill—God's Kingdom. But why are you failing in life? Why are you not fulfilling as demanded?

*"Therefore my people are gone into captivity, because they have no knowledge: and their honorable men are famished, and their multitude dried up with thirst. Therefore hell hath enlarged herself, and opened her mouth without measure: and their glory, and their multitude and their pomp, and he that rejoiceth, shall descend into it. And the mean man shall be brought down, and the mighty man shall be humbled, and the eyes of the lofty shall be humbled"* (Isaiah 5:13-14)

Nothing frustrates or destroys like ignorance! If you don't know who you are, your life will produce negative fruits. The word **'hell'** here means anguish. To be dried up with thirst is to be in lack. May you not be humiliated in life!

It is definite that your personal ambition will stagger if it is not God's plan for you. You could be rejoicing, but you will soon know that there is no future for what you are doing, if it is a mere ambition.

*"Many plans are in a man's mind, but it is the Lord's purpose for him that will stand"* (Proverbs 19:21 Amp)

Stop pursuing ambition(s) as a man chasing the wind. The world is full of people that are certified on certain courses by virtue of education; but today, they found themselves locating fulfillment and peace as God led them into another area of life they never thought of.

*"As he approached Jerusalem and saw the city, he wept over it and said, If you, even you, had only known on this thy day what would bring you peace but now it is hidden from your eyes"* (Luke 19:41-42)

I want you to go to God in prayer and let him show you what your peace is tied onto. Nevertheless, you are the reason why this book is written. I see you emerging a happy person as you read this book to the end in Jesus' name!

# CHAPTER ONE

## UNDERSTANDING YOUR INDIVIDUALITY

IT IS VERY EASY to react over any name a man calls you, when you do not know what your make-up is. It is easy to behave like a screwdriver, whereas, you are made a spanner. If you lack the understanding of your make-up, you are bound to respond to any name people call you.

It will take only the manufacturer of a product to tell what a product is. That is why we have a manual attached to any expensive and valuable products to enable the users understand the way the product functions. This manual is called, **"The manufacturer's mind".**

## DISCOVERING YOUR DIVINE DESIGN (MAKE-UP)

If you really want to know your make-up, you need to go to God, the sole manufacturer of your life. If you are not born again, it will be difficult for God to relate any matter to you because you will not understand him; for your spirit is not alive towards God.

When Adam sinned, something happened in him. He died spiritually; hence, everyone that is not born again carries the nature of the fallen Adam by birth because we were all generated after his kind until Christ came. This is why, when God speaks to a sinner, he or she may not hear him nor understand him, because God's word is spiritually discerned

(1Corinthians 2:14). But when you are born again, your spirit that died in Adam comes alive. It is only then you can relate with God by your spirit. For the bible says:

*"But there is a spirit in man: and the inspiration of the Almighty giveth them understanding"* (Job 32:8)

## HOW OUR SPIRIT DIED IN ADAM

When God was to make man, he said, *"Let us make man in our own image."* So, man is a spirit being, who has a soul (life) and lives in the body—the only natural house where God put him. Man was put in the body to enable and qualify him to relate with the earth because the body was made out of the earth. (It is illegal to nature for spirit to live here on earth, except through a physical body.) That is why it takes physical food to maintain the body, and spiritual food (God's word) to maintain the spirit-man (Deuteronomy. 8:3).

After creation, God commanded man to reproduce after his kind. So, when the life of the spirit-man died as a result of spoilage through using wrong substance on it—disobedience, Adam began to reproduce dead spirit-men in his kind after his fall. That is why the Bible says, *"For all have sinned and fall short of the glory of God"* (Rom. 3:23).

This is why everybody became dead in the spirit.

## YOU CAN COME ALIVE AGAIN

*"For by one man's offence death reigned by one; much more they which receive abundance of grace and of the gift of righteousness shall reign in life by one, Jesus Christ. Therefore as the offence of one, judgment came upon all men to condemnation; even so by the righteousness of one the free gift came upon all men unto justification of life. For as by one man's disobedience many were made sinners, so by the obedience of one shall many be made righteous?"* (Romans 5: 17-19)

*"That as sin hath reigned unto death, even so might grace reign through righteousness unto eternal life by Jesus Christ our Lord"* (Romans 5:21)

*"There is therefore now no condemnation to them which are in Christ Jesus, who walk not after the flesh, but after the Spirit. For the law of the spirit of life in Christ Jesus hath made me free from the law of sin and death"* (Romans 8:1, 2)

So, receiving Jesus into you, as your life and personal savior, is the only healing that can bring life back to your spirit by displacement—the law (power) of the spirit of life in Christ Jesus displacing and replacing the law (power) of sin and death in you. This way, you can come alive again. This is called '**Born-again experience**'.

*"And this is the record that God hath given to us eternal life, and this life is in his Son. He that hath the Son hath life; and he that hath not the Son of God hath not life"* (1 John 5:11, 12)

## HOW CAN IT HAPPEN?

*"But what saith it? The word is nigh thee, even in thy mouth, and in thine heart: that is, the word of faith, which we preach; that if thou shalt confess with thy mouth the Lord Jesus, and shalt believe in thine heart that God hath raised him from the dead, thou shalt be saved. For with the heart man believeth unto righteousness; and with the mouth confession is made unto salvation"* (Romans 10:8-10)

*"For by grace are ye saved through faith; and that not of yourself; it is the gift of God"* (Ephesians 2:8)

*"For God so loved the world, that He gave His only begotten Son, that whosoever believeth in Him should not perish, but have everlasting life"* (John 3:16)

It is that simple. Just believe that he died for you to deliver you from **'Adamic sin'.** As you follow the rules of salvation by the scriptures you've just read, may you come alive again in your spirit to enable you relate with God in Jesus' name!

If you are not born again, why not repeat this prayer after me now:

*"Lord Jesus, have mercy on me. Forgive me my sins. Wash me with your blood. Deliver me from the kingdom of Satan into your Kingdom. And*

3

*come into my life. I accept you as my Lord and personal Savior in Jesus' precious name! Amen."*

Now, you are saved, if you said this prayer with me. Hallelujah!

## YOU ARE FULL OF VALUE

When God was creating the heavens and the earth, he only spoke a word and then it came to pass. But when it came to creating man, God had to settle down. Man is the duplicate of God Himself. Man has a specific uniqueness, even from each other (Psalm.139: 14-16; Romans 12:4-8; 1Corinthians 12:14-26).

In the first place, man has dominion over his environment (Psalm 8: 4-8; Genesis 1: 26, 27).

Secondly, he has dominion over life.

As no member of the body is to be despised, so is no human on earth is to be treated with contempt. Your importance is not attached to your status, race, or stature; not even your educational or family background. It is attached to the potential(s), talent(s), gift(s) or abilities within you.

You are a benefit to your generation. You are carrying what your world is in need of. You are a debtor to your generation. If you die without benefiting your generation, a stillborn child is better than you (that is, a child born dead). The reason why you were born before the coming generation is because you could be a pacesetter, just like Jacob and Joseph.

*"The Lord sent a word into Jacob, and it hath lighted upon Israel"* (Isaiah 9:8)

This is to imply that only one idea God gave to Jacob affected his whole generation positively. What about Joseph?

*"He sent a man before them, even Joseph, who was sold for a servant"* (Psalm 105:17)

You have a placement here on earth for the oncoming generation and for the present one. Also, Jesus said, **"Occupy till I come"**. This means that you are born to occupy a certain position here on earth. You are not entitled to go to grave with all your abilities and potentials untapped.

Always remember this: you are the missing ingredient in the soup of your generation. Your world is in need of you. You are an embodiment of God's praise to your world. Your death will mean much of a great loss to the world at large. You are a full package of blessings to this world. Life will reward you according to the color you will add to it. The expertise of your nation towards other nations of the world depends on the trading of your talent and calling in life. The importance of your potential(s) cannot be over-emphasized. The world is searching for what is waiting to be manifested out of you. So, do not put her (the world) in the dark eternally. Discover yourself!

The greatest discovery in life is the discovery of oneself—what he/she carries. The greatest miracle the world needs today is the miracle of the mind—insight.

*"The eyes of your understanding being enlightened; that ye may know what is the hope of his calling, and what are the riches of the glory of the inheritance in the saints"* (Ephesians 1:18)

The devil has taken the duty upon him to be blinding the understanding of people, thereby making them to be ignorant to their personalities.

One of the principles of the mind is that what you see with it will determine what you believe, and that is what you act out of you. This is why the devil will always want to turn away your mental eyes to negative things about yourself and cause you to hate your existence. May God deliver you (if you are in such condition) today! For you to begin to see your true self, I pray that every negative scale covering your mental eyes should fall off now in Jesus' name!

Know this: you are not made to be a burden but a blessing to your generation. God has carefully packaged you as a blessing. So, wake up. Do you not know that your spiritual awakening today will effect a change in the predicament, reproach or shame that is bastardizing your society, nation or the world at large? I see your world beginning to look for you!

Let me add this to your understanding: you don't have your like in this world. You are a unique being. Nobody can exchange you nor even be able to step in your shoes in life. If you don't know your worth, then it suggests that you are worthless.

*"Man that is in honour, and understandeth not, is like the beasts that perish"* (Psalm 49:20)

I want to let you know that you are not just occupying a space in this world; you have a duty to offer your generation. You are highly needed in life. Please sell your services for the success of others.

# DANGER OF MISUNDERSTANDING ONE'S MAKE-UP

Individual malfunctioning is a product of self-misunderstanding. If you don't know your real use, you will be abused. That is, you will be abnormally used. This is why people work in a wrong company, do the wrong job or be in the wrong place and will never have joy, satisfaction nor real peace and fulfillment in their lives and homes. As you are reading this book I see you liberated in Jesus' name!

If you sell off your real God-given personal idea about yourself and buy the ideas of people about you, you enroll into the University of Failure in life.

Many of you are still being tied to your past memory of ridicules, mockeries and intimidations from your parents, friends or relatives. Nobody really knows you. Take example from the case of Jesus:

*"When Jesus came into the coasts of Caesarea Philippi, he asked his disciples, saying, Whom do men say that I the Son of man am? And they said, Some say that thou art John the Baptist: some Elias; and others, Jeremiah, or one of the prophets. He saith unto them, But who say ye that I am? And Simon Peter answered and said, Thou art the Christ, the Son of the living God. And Jesus answered and said unto him, Blessed art thou, Simon Bar-Jonah:*

*for flesh and blood hath not revealed it unto thee but my Father which is in heaven"* (Matthew 16:13-17)

It will take God, who is your Manufacturer, to show you who you really are. Nobody can interpret you accurately. So, if you don't have the understanding of who you are, you will lose your self-respect, dignity and persuasive personality. And if this happens, you will lack a sense of duty or stewardship to your generation. Certain defects like inferiority complex will set in; confusion of the mind will be your next door neighbor.

When I talk about your make-up, I mean what God has made you to be in life. Are you a doctor, pastor, evangelist, teacher, leader, a military man, a policeman, a lawyer, a scientist, etc.? See what God told Jeremiah:

*"Before I formed thee in the belly I knew thee; and before thou camest forth out of the womb I sanctified thee, and I ordained thee a prophet unto the nations"* (Jeremiah 1:5)

God is not the person that made you, if you have no purpose or fashion. Everything he made has a form; so, why not you?

If you don't know your person, your sense of value will be gone; self-intimidation and limitation will arrive in your life, your steps may lose speed in the race of life. Life to you may become a burden or a bond of frustration and you will be tossed to and fro by every wind of opportunity or employment.

A man who knows who he is never settles for just any kind of activity. You can't find him in the midst of mediocrities. He is always a costly commodity. You can't price him cheaply. You don't talk to him anyhow. A high value is placed upon him; he is always a man of high premium and reputation. So, you have to find out your value and what it is attached to.

God says, *"Their honourable men became famished . . ."* This means that there are people that are termed nonentities in this world that have values and honor undiscovered. **"Man that is in honour, and understandeth not, is like the beasts that perish."** (Psalms 49:20)

May God open your eyes today in Jesus' name!

Because you don't know who you are, that is why you don't know the right job you should give yourself to.

Please note what I want to tell you now: without discovering yourself, you will never know the right wife to marry. Every beautiful, respectful and admirable girl, whose make-up may not fit into yours and your destiny, will attract you.

A wife is supposed to be a help-meet (somebody who is qualified to help you fulfill your calling in life, and not a liability). It is the same in the other way round.

If you don't know your design, you will never know what course to study in school.

Because many people don't know who they are, they do not know the right career to pursue. Many are too sentimental or are always being carried away by companies' jobs that do not match with their ability. If you know you are a musician or a footballer by divine design, why not go for it? Why would you squeeze yourself into a hole you are not fit for, comparing yourself with another? Don't do anything you are never made for, no matter the pressure of people on you. If you do, you are only going to shorten your life span because; it will bring you depression and struggle without a successful result.

Imagine a situation where, in football game, Number Two will be put in the position of Number Ten. That is total foolishness and stupidity of the highest order.

You will even break the law of relationship when you don't know your make-up. I believe you understand that birds of same feathers flock together. An eagle can never be found flying in oneness with a group of pigeons. This is because it will lose its place as the king of the birds. It will lose its worth and it will lose its name as an eagle. In fact, to be blind to oneself is to be enslaved by another. May you regain your position in life right now!

# HOW CAN YOU UNDERSTAND YOUR MAKE-UP?

*"It is the glory of God to conceal a thing: but the honour of kings is to search out a matter"* (Proverbs 25:2)

Your honor is attached to your value.

'Kings' simply means, in the above scripture, a great man. Your greatness is attached to what God has created you to do as a solution to a particular problem in your time. So your ability to search it out makes you a king to your world. If you don't really know who you are and God is truly your manufacturer, and you really know it, there should not be any question about who you are in your heart any more. Just find out from him.

The Bible says, in 1 Peter 1:25 that Jesus is the Shepherd and Bishop of your soul, who knows everything about you and the way your life should go. So, in order to know your make-up, the following steps will guide you:

1. Be willing to know it
2. Pour out your soul and call upon God. He is your manufacturer (Jeremiah 33:3)

God is saying, **"Come, let me show you who you really are. Your opinion about yourself could be wrong. So consult me and I will show or reveal yourself to you."**

See what the Psalmist said,

*"For thou hast possessed my reins: thou hast covered me in my mother's womb. I will praise thee; for I am fearfully and wonderfully made: marvellous are thy works; and that my soul knoweth right well. My substance was not hid from thee, when I was made in secret, and curiously wrought in the lowest parts of the earth. Thine eyes did see my substance, yet being unperfect; and in thy book all my members were written, which in continuance were fashioned, when as yet there was none of them"* (Psalm 139:13-16)

Everything about you is in God's book. He carefully planned your design before he manufactured you. So, let the Holy Spirit reveal who you really are to you from God's book.

When Jesus asked the disciples of what people say about him or who he is in Matthew 16:13-17, nobody could give him the correct answer except Peter. And Jesus said, *"Flesh and blood did not reveal it to you but my Father who is in heaven."* So go before God in prayers of enquiry. He will definitely show you your real make-up!

He said,

*"Then shall ye call upon me, and ye shall go and pray unto me, and I will hearken unto you. And ye shall seek me, and find me, when ye shall search for me with all your heart"* (Jeremiah.29: 12-13).

He also went on to say, *"Call unto me, and I will answer thee, and shew thee great and mighty things, which thou knowest not"* (Jeremiah 33:3)

May God show you his faithfulness by revealing your make-up to you! May you be free from confusion of the mind! I see you having peace. I see you regaining your worth. I see you regaining your self-value. I see no man ridiculing you anymore in life. I see you finding dignity again in the name of Jesus!

# CHAPTER TWO

## UNDERSTANDING YOUR PURPOSE OR ASSIGNMENT

WHAT IS "PURPOSE?" PURPOSE is the reason why something was made or designed to function in a particular way. I will give more definition of purpose as we continue, but let me begin this chapter by talking about **"The Law of Destiny."**

**"The Law of Destiny"** states that a man's life depends on his purpose, timing and geographical location; and until these three factors are in place, your life will not be fulfilled.

A man without a purpose or who has no knowledge of his divine purpose is like a man who just joined a car on the road, knowing neither the direction of the car nor his personal direction; or a man who gets on the highway just going nowhere.

I also liken the man who does not know his divine purpose to a man who was sent on an errand that got to the middle of the journey and his cell phone got lost without his knowledge. The cell phone is supposed to be the only point of contact between him and his boss. When he arrived at his destination, he forgot the content of his assignment. Dipping his hand into his pocket for his cell phone, he discovered that it had been lost. All that such a man needs to do is to go back to his boss and start all over again.

The bible says in Psalm 82:5, *"They know not, neither will they understand, they walk on in darkness: all the foundations of the earth are out of course"* (Psalm 82:5).

Many people are living in ignorance. It is better for you to know your purpose than wandering in your mind on what to do, just as the bible says in Ecclesiastes 6:9a: *"Better is the sight of the eyes than the wandering of desire: this is also vanity and vexation of spirit"* (Ecclesiastes 6:9).

## YOUR DESTINY IS NOT YOUR DECISION

God is the author and finisher of your destiny. He is the Alpha and the Omega, the beginning and the end of your life. He is the only one that can show you your destiny. As far as he is your manufacturer, he is the only one that can show you what you are fashioned to do.

Look at what the Bible says: *"Man's goings are of the Lord; how can a man then understand his own way?"* (Proverbs 20:24).

*"Oh Lord, I know that the way of man is not in himself: it is not in man that walketh to direct his steps"* (Jeremiah 10:23)

*"Come now, you who say, Today or tomorrow we will go to such and such a city, spend a year there, buy and sell, and make a profit; Whereas you do not know what will happen tomorrow. For what is your life? It is even a vapour that appears for a little time and then vanishes away. Instead you ought to say, If the Lord wills, we shall live and do this or that. But now you boast in your arrogance. All such boasting is evil"* (James 4:13-16)

You may decide to follow your own plan; but no matter your financial success, if there is no divine peace, satisfaction, true happiness and personal fulfillment in your life, you are not on divine purpose.

Life is not all about accumulation of wealth. You are not sent to this earth to pursue personal ambition(s). If at the end of the day, you get to heaven without the achievement of your purpose, you will answer query before God.

Before you were born, there is a particular problem you are designed to solve. You are an instrument of change to your society.

Prosperity is defined as having God's enough provision for your assignment. So, stop pursuing food and shelter in vain without purpose in your life. All these things are just but a common shadow that will soon fade away. They are only meant to maintain and sustain your stay here on earth. Hallelujah! Remember, you will leave them very soon. Therefore, please, locate your purpose and fulfill it before you leave this earth. Every blessing that is allowed to come your way is a provision for your possible stay on earth, and a reward for selling what you have from divinity to your generation.

A stillborn child is better than an eighty-year-old man who does not know his purpose. He is like a confusion going somewhere to happen.

A man without a purpose is like someone traveling without direction and compass on the sea, in the air, or on land that got to a junction and became confused. He could be angry and bitter in heart. He could even become critical. He may begin to live his life by destroying others.

Your purpose is your dream that God gave to you to bring to fruition. Every man has a divine road to walk on; so, find out your own.

Paul said, *"I therefore so run, not as uncertainty; so fight I not as one that beateth the air"* (1 Corinthians 9:26). Solomon the wise man also said, *"A man void of understanding striketh hands, and becometh surety in the present of his friends"* (Proverbs 17: 18).

God is not happy about how people have spoilt his plans by going for their own ambitions. So God has to go against the plans of so many men and women, including nations, in order to bring his own plan to pass.

*"The Lord bringeth the counsel of the heathen to naught: he maketh the devices of the people of none effect. The counsel of the Lord standeth forever, the thoughts of his heart to all generation"* (Psalm33:10, 11)

This is one of the major reasons why your plans are not working out for you, thereby making you jump from one idea to another. You can't swim against a-fast-moving water. That is what many people are doing with their lives. Your purpose is God's project; you are just an instrument with which God would bring it to pass.

A man who understands his purpose never worries in life. He is like someone working in a company. Everything about his assignment is to be provided for by the company—security, financial support, accommodation and mobility. So is the case of a man on purpose;

1.   God makes sure he is provided with everything he needs. Everything Jesus needed to fulfill his earthly ministry was provided for; even Prophet Moses experienced the same.

2.   God makes sure he never struggles. The Bible says, *"For by strength shall no man prevail"* (1 Samuel 2:9b).

*"So then it is not of him that willeth, nor of him that runneth, but of God that sheweth mercy"* (Romans 9:16)

*"I return, and saw under the sun, that the race is not to the swift, nor the battle to the strong, neither yet bread to the wise, nor yet riches to men of understanding, nor yet favour to men of skill; but time and chance happeneth to them all"* (Ecclesiastes 9:11)

*". . . not by might, nor by power, but by my Spirit, saith the Lord of host. The hands of Zerubbabel have laid the foundation of this house; his hands shall also finish it . . ."* (Zechariah 4:6; 9)

3.   Doors open everywhere God leads him to and enemies give way for him because God has made him his sanctuary and partner.

*"When Israel came out of Egypt, the house of Jacob from a people of strange language, Judah became God's sanctuary (the Holy place of His habitation) and Israel His dominion (Exodus 29:45, 46; Deut, 27:9), the red sea looked and fled; the Jordan (River) was turned back (Exodus 14:21; Joshua 3:13, 16; Psalm 77:16). The mountains skipped like rams, the little hills like lambs"* (Psalm 114:1-4, AMP)

4.   He will be highly protected by God. God's anointing and favor follow him, and his enemies will be completely helpless.

*"You prepare a table before me in the presence of my enemies. You anoint my head with oil, my brimming cup runs over. Surely or only goodness and mercy, and unfailing love shall follow me all the days of my life . . ."* (Psalm 23:5-6, AMP)

5. He receives divine direction.

*"And thine ears shall hear a word behind thee, saying, this is the way, walk ye in it, when ye turn to the right hand, and when ye turn to the left"* (Isaiah 30:21)

*"I will instruct thee and teach in the way which thou shalt go: I will guide thee with mine eyes"* (Psalm 32:8)

6. Because God leads him, prosperity becomes his portion.

*"Thus says the Lord, your redeemer, the Holy one of Israel: I am the Lord Your God, who teaches you to profit, who leads you in the way that you should go. Oh, that you had hearkened to my commandment! Then your peace and prosperity would have been like a flowing river . . ."* (Isaiah 48:17, 18 AMP)

7. God makes sure he reaches the high places of the earth (the place of influence, affluence and prominence)

*"He found him in a desert land, and in the waste howling wilderness; he led him about he instructed him, he kept him as the apple of his eye . . . he made him ride on the high places of the earth, that he might eat the increase of the fields"* (Deuteronomy 32:10, 13)

8. God is always with him, speaking to him to ensure his courage and confidence

*"Fear not (there is nothing to fear), for I am with you; do not look around you in tumor and be dismayed, for I am your God. I will strengthen and harden you against difficulties, yes, I will help you; yes, I will hold you up and retain you with my (victorious) right hand of righteousness and justice. Behold all they who are enraged and inflamed against you shall be put to*

*shame and confounded; they who strive against you shall be as nothing and shall perish"* (Isaiah 41:10-11, AMP)

*"But if you will indeed listen to and obey His voice and all that I speak, then I will be an enemy to your enemies and an adversary to your adversaries"* (Exodus 23:22)

This is because he is going after the very heart-beat of God. So God must surely be for him (Romans 8:31). May you be connected to your divine purpose in the name of Jesus!

## WHY YOU MUST KNOW YOUR DIVINE PURPOSE

Oh, yes! It is expedient for you to know your purpose because it is the myth behind success. It is the pivot around which your whole life revolves. It is the divine instruction to which your heavenly provision and divine backing is tied to. As soon as you lay your hand on it, your life begins a positive journey. This is called '**The turning moment of a divine success**'.

Success is not an accumulation of financial and material wealth. These are not good factors for measuring success. Success is known as the step-by-step achievement of your divine goal.

There is something in your hand that your generation demands. Life is all about stewardship—servicing the needs of others. Your ultimate value in life is measured by your value to your generation. The true life spam of a man is not his chronological age. It is measured by the service he rendered to his generation. Your destiny will never see greatness until you are prepared to service the needs of your fellow human beings. Seek the well-being of your fellows. As for the position you are occupying in life, either in government, company, industry or organization, you are there for the well-being of others to which you are assigned.

Because success begins at a point with the oversight of an end, your purpose therefore has an end. When you leave this world, you will give an account of your assignment to God. When you die, your biography will either be filled with the measure of your accumulation of wealth or the measure of the humble service(s) you rendered, so as to bring about positive change(s) to the lives of people.

We have three kinds of success in life:

1.   Human success: it is based on human principles, traditions and methods. It is self-centered. It gives no room for others. The driving force for human success is 'Self'. It is characterized with struggle. It leads to self-glory. It has the following in its circle:

a.   Thieves
b.   Cheaters
c.   Tricksters

Those are violators of human rights.

2.   Satanic success: it is based on contrary things against God's mind. Its common motto is: **"The way up is pulling others down."** Satan is the originator of this. The people under this category are those committing murder in the name of, **"I must make it in life"**, not thinking about life beyond. But remember, *"There is a way which seemeth right unto a man, but the end thereof are the ways of death"* **(Proverbs 14:12).**

*"What shall it profit a man if he shall gain the whole world and lose his soul"* (Mark 8:36)

3.   Divine covenant success: it is based on God's principles, driven by God's will and monitored by God's word. (Isaiah 48:17; Psalm 1:1-3; Joshua 1:8). Its major target is to expand the Kingdom of God.

*"Cry yet, saying, Thus saith the Lord of host; My cities through prosperity shall yet be spread abroad . . ."* (Zechariah 1:17)

So it is expedient for you to carry a sense of purpose. Why Jesus succeeded in finishing his work on earth through the Cross as purposed for him was because he had a sense of purpose

He said, *"The Spirit of the Lord is upon me, because he hath anointed me to preach the gospel to the poor; he hath sent me to heal the broken hearted, to preach deliverance to the captives, and recovering of sight to the blind, to set at liberty them that are bruised"* (Luke 4:18).

That was his mission statement!

*"In the mean while his disciples prayed him, saying, Master, eat. But he said unto them, I have meat to eat that ye know not of. Therefore, said the disciples one to another, Hath any man brought him ought to eat? Jesus said unto them, My meat is to do the will of him that sent, me and to finish his work"* (John 4:31-34)

The following reasons for knowing your purpose will keep you from human or satanic success in life:

1.  Life without purpose is a bond of frustration. This is the genesis of worry and anxiety.

Paul said, *"I therefore so run, not as uncertainly; so fight I, not as one that beateth the air"* (1 Corinthians 9:26).

King Solomon also made the same statement. He said, *"A man void of understanding striketh hands, and becometh surety in the presence of his friend" (Proverbs 17:18).* And he also added to it, saying, *"Better is the sight of the eyes than the wandering of desire: this is vanity and vexation of the spirit"* (Ecclesiastes 6:9).

A life of trial and error without result in life leads to frustration and weariness. I pray that God will give you direction in the name of Jesus!

2.  Purpose gives room for concentration/focus.

Jesus said, *"Now is my soul troubled; and what shall I say? Father; save me from this hour: but for this cause came I unto this hour"* (John 12:27).

That is to say, even when it became almost difficult to go to the Cross, he was still focused, never willing to give up because he knew his purpose. Even when people wanted him to remain in a particular place, especially Peter and his group, who never fully understood Jesus' calling at that time, came to tell him the mind of the people, saying,

". . . *All men seek for thee where you preached before*" (Mark. 1:37, Paraphrased)

But Jesus answering, said unto him,

"*. . . Let us go unto the next towns, that I may preach there also for therefore came I forth*" (Mark 1:38).

This is purely an understanding of one's purpose. May God open your eyes of understanding to know why you came forth to this earth also in Jesus' name!

3.  It will help you to do the right thing and not just anything that seems good. This will make you to always be in the centre of God's will. Jesus knew this. The bible says, "*Then those men, when they had seen the miracle that Jesus did, said, This is of a truth, that prophet that should come into the world. When Jesus therefore perceived that they would come and take him by force, to make him a king, he departed again into a mountain himself*" (John 6:14, 15).

Until you know your purpose, you will never understand the distractions that the devil will bring your way, but will always mistake distractions for opportunities. May God give you understanding!

4.  It will help you change the story of your family's (poor) background. When you discover God's divine purpose for your life, your life will regain its originality and direction. God becomes committed to you financially and otherwise.

Purpose terminates mockery and poverty in a man's life. This is because God is behind all divine purposes, and without him, you can do nothing (I Sam. 2:6-10, Ecclesiastes 3:14, 11; Psalm 146:5; 27:10, Romans 9:16; 1 Thessalonians 5:18, Zechariah 4:6).

Even the story of Jesus, who is our Master, was changed, when great things started to happen. He was even more honored than the kings of his time. He came out of Nazareth, a place with no positive historical recognition (John 1:46), but His purpose changed them all.

What about Peter? A common fisherman, who later became a great preacher with great miracles? (Acts 9:36-42; 32-35; 4:14-16). Purpose will surely change the trend of your history. May you have a new story too as you attend to your divine purpose in the name of Jesus!

When God's instruction, tagged with God's promises, comes to you, you become vital, no matter your past. It will boost your understanding about life. That is, it will revitalize, transform, remodel and re-pattern your mind and sense of reasoning. You no longer think like an indigent fellow or a mediocre. The thought of greatness is what it impacts if you believe in the instruction and the promises behind it; and if you believe that God will bring his word to pass.

Moses was a common shepherd, who only reasoned like a shepherd, but when he found God's purpose for his life, he became a god to Pharaoh and the president of a whole nation with about three million (3.000.000) people. He was specially designed to bring God's people out of the land of bondage. This assignment changed his thought pattern. Wonderful! That is the same way God will change whatever name people have ever called you to 'Success', beginning from now!

5.   Purpose will keep you from wastages and unnecessary expenditures. It will make you to wisely prioritize your income, especially to the most necessities according to the order of importance:

a.)   Books and lectures for more information. Most people waste too much money on fashion than other things that are basic in life and at the end they will have no money to pursue their divine purpose. This is one of the causes of failure. Be disciplined!

b.)   Life's basic necessities, etc.

6.   It will make you know the right course to study at school.

Listen; that you studied in one of the best schools in your state or country or any part of the world is not the ultimate in life. That is not what purpose is. You may attend the best school in the world and still be a perfect failure. No school will offer you success principles or certificate. Even if they do, it will never define your success in life because you may still study and be certified on a wrong track of life. Locate your purpose and study for it.

7.   It will make you know or recognize who your spouse should be; not by color, stature, economic or social status.

So many females marry husbands that they don't know where the car of their lives is heading to, and many marry wives that are not fit to help them. But when you know your divine purpose, you will be able to identify the person that can share your pains and joys with you; and that can be the best person to encourage you when you fall (Ecclesiastes 4:9-12). I adjure you to marry someone who understands your purpose and have interest in what you are born to do; or else, you will experience the major regret of your life when nobody, including your wife or husband, is ready to encourage you on what you find peace, joy and fulfillment in, when doing it.

A man of God came to my hometown, Umutu, in Delta State, Nigeria, to preach in a crusade, and publicly declared his wife as unfruitful to him in the area of ministry. Another Pastor's wife divorced him in the middle of marital life. What a pain of the soul! May God never let you into this kind of unforgettable misery!

8.   It will make you recognize your true friends, for not everybody is your friend. You can't be a mechanical engineer and be a best friend to a medical doctor. What will be the trend of your discussions?

Your friend is someone who adds to what you are, and not who reduces you or discourages your right decisions based on your purpose.

9.   The sense of purpose helps you to know the books to read, the right media to watch and the audio to listen to.

A man's life is a product of information and experience gathered into him. The direction of your life is determined by what you hear and what you see daily.

When your mind has gathered information, it will metamorphose into a belief. Belief is a product of the mind formed by a long-term meditation and understanding.

When information has come to the point of belief, they have no option than to be transmuted into their physical equivalence through the members of your body. So your life must go in the direction of your belief because, a message, after passing through a critical assessment and it is agreed upon, will be passed from your conscious mind into your subconscious mind. And your subconscious mind has no ability to judge it but will only pass it into your feelings, and then your feelings will definitely produce actions. That is why Jesus said, *"Out of the abundance of the heart the mouth speaketh"* (Matthew 12:34b).

See the process in James 1:13-15.

So when your mind has been filled with certain information to its boiling point, you have no more will power to refrain from doing it because the vapor must be released. You must guide your life by majoring on the things that concern your purpose.

*"Keep thy heart with all diligence; for out of it are the issues of life"* (Proverbs 4:23)

I see you succeeding! May your feet be consciously guided speedily in life in the mighty name of Jesus!

10.  A sense of purpose passes into you a proper understanding of your life by helping you to know who you are, whom you are, where you came from (heaven), where you are going in life, and what you are really born to do.

11.  It will give you direction in life and make life meaningful and enjoyable to you. It will even make you find the earth as a suitable place to dwell and give you a sense of managing your life in order to prolong your days. In fact, when you find purpose, you will be tempted to pray to God for Christ to stay more years before coming, because life will be so pleasing to you. No wonder Hezekiah asked for more days! You will live long for the benefit of your generation in Jesus' name!

Look at God's promise for you: *"Whereas thou hast been forsaken and hated, so that no man went through thee, I will make thee an eternal Excellency, a joy of many generations"* (Isaiah 60:15).

Your generation will be missing you when you die. No wonder some people cry so painfully when someone that is so dear to them dies. May God keep you for us!

12. Purpose gives you an assurance of a good future and terminates the fear of uncertainty in your life, and it will also remove stagnation, frustration and confusion from your life. It will give you a good definition of what your life is and give you a settled mind.

13. As a solution carrier, it will help you to know the kind of problem you are born to solve in this would. This will help you not to lay your hand on just anything kind of job, and help you to stop wandering about, looking for casual jobs (white collar jobs). Also, it will help you to maximize your seasons profitably in life.

14. It will help you to be conscious of the **"Law of Time"** and the **"Law of Geography"**. This will be explained in chapter ten, under **"The Governing Laws of Nature"**. Your life will be manifested phase by phase because God has programmed it to be so. You will never be allowed to enter into your next phase until the duty of your present phase has ended, no matter how you pray. It is written, saying, *"To everything there is a season, and a time to every purpose under the heaven"* (Ecclesiastes 3:1).

Job, who had struggled in many ways to be better in life and had more experiences in life more than many of us made us to know that every change in our lives is programmed in seasons.

*". . . all the days of my appointed time will I wait till my change come"* (Job 14:14)

This is because he knew that **"It is neither by power nor by might"**, and **"by strength shall no man prevail."**

It is also noted that your life has a destined place for maximum fulfillment. Where you are sent is where you will succeed. Remember

Isaac (Genesis 26:1-3; 12-14)! Remember Jesus (Luke 9:51-53). Remember Jonah (Jonah 1:1-17).

Until these three things—purpose, time for purpose, and purpose's divine geographical location—are in place, you will never find a maximum fulfillment, if you will ever find any fulfillment at all. In fact, your greatest mistake will happen if you hurry. A wise man said, "Life is a marathon, not a fifty-yard dash". Jesus never hurried; even when he had been seeing the sick, oppressed, etc. until his time came.

15. Purpose will provide opportunities and promotions for you in life. Remember Joseph (Genesis 41:1-57).

16. Purpose produces the zeal for a continuous move. With purpose, you will not be easily discouraged in life (Isaiah 9:6, 7).

17. Understanding Purpose will give you the courage to move toward oppositions and conquer them with holy aggression, no matter how big they look.

Samuel anointed David to be king. After that, it was noised that a strong man from Philistine, called Goliath, was breathing out threat against Israel. And again, it was announced that whoever killed him would be the next king, and that the king's daughter would be given to him for wife. Wow! What a shortcut and a wonderful privilege for David! (David took advantage of it, of course!

Now listen, or else you make a terrible error by imitation. In Joel 2:7, 8, the Bible says that on your way to success in life, every problem you meet is not designed to kill you but for you to solve it to work out your lifting.

The reason why nobody could go after Goliath was because they were not made to solve such problem. It was meant for only David. I believe God Himself programmed it. May God help you to know the problem(s) that demand your attention, so you can avoid generating problems toward yourself.

18. Your blessings in life are tied to your purpose. Leaving it for another thing or personal ambition will make you lose color in life.

*"He that tilleth his land shall be satisfied with bread . . ."* (Proverbs 12:11)

Take note that it did not say *"He that tilleth another man's land"*. This land signifies your purpose. Find out your land, therefore, to avoid wasting your precious time and energy. May God help you!

19. Your grace and ability to function effectively in life are tied to your divine purpose (Romans 12:3-8). So if you are a **'leg'**, you better have to be a **'leg'** to enable you to do what a leg can do. Remember, a hand cannot do the function of a leg. So understand who you are and what you can do in life, and stop being sentimental. Don't choose a career just for a show-off.

20. It reduces your prayer points from unreasonable requests to thanksgiving, knowing that God is the author and finisher of your life (Jeremiah 1:5; 1 Thessalonians 5: 24; Philippians 1: 6).

21. When you are on purpose, anytime you reason along the track of your purpose, ideas (knowledge and wisdom) beam to you as a light from heaven, giving you direction and making you creative; thereby, making you excellent in your area of calling.

22. Purpose separates you from unnecessary things and from unwanted multitudes, helping you to focus and surround yourself with wise people within your area of endeavor. For the bible says, *"Through desire a man, having separated himself, seeketh and intermeddleth with all wisdom"* (Proverbs 18: 1).

23. Your life will not be hard for you, if you pursue your purpose of existence here on earth (Matthew 25: 14-30).

**"Gnashing of teeth"** in the above scriptures means hard life, while **"total darkness"** means obscured life. This is my personal view of those Scriptures.

24. Your purpose is what God will anoint you for. Jesus enumerated the reasons for his anointing in Luke 4:18, showing us that God cannot anoint someone without a reason.

To be anointed is to be empowered for a mission to your generation. This is called an impartation of divine ability.

You will not suffer! I see your understanding opened in the mighty name of Jesus!

With these reasons, if you have not located your purpose, begin now to negotiate with God concerning your purpose. God cannot waste his precious time, resources and energy creating you just for nothing. You are not a biological accident; and you can never be one. You are highly priced. You are too precious in God's sight and to humanity. You are the workmanship of God (Ephesians 2: 10). Do not let anyone intimidate you. Find out your usefulness to your generation.

# YOU, YOUR ASSIGNMENT AND THE HOLY SPIRIT

*"For as many as are led by the Spirit of God, they are the sons of God"* (Romans 8:14)

To be led by the Holy Spirit is to be led by God.

I want to show you the role of the Holy Spirit in your life and purpose. If you don't walk with the Holy Spirit after discovering the vision of your purpose, you will personally fill your divine purpose with your own ambitions. This is where many fail in their pursuit of purpose.

Divine purpose, if pursued with divine instructions on a daily basis will lead to divine success. You will not fail!

### Why you must walk with the Holy Spirit in your life

As far as you are made human, you remain imperfect; and so you are bound to make mistakes in life. You need a perfect God to guide you perfectly into your fulfillment. Divine destiny is not carnal nor to be pursued carnally. As far as it is from God, who is a Spirit, it must be pursued spiritually by being sensitive to the Holy Spirit so that one would not miss the whole thing on the way.

The Bible says, *"The foolishness of a man perverted his way: and his heart fretteth against the Lord"* (Proverbs 19:3).

Life is full of so many who have made terrible mistakes in their lives based on ignorance of their personal foolishness in pursuing their destinies humanly; yet, all blames go to God.

Now, let's look at the reasons why you must walk with the Holy Spirit:

1.  The Holy Spirit created you. He was among the spiritual entities that made you during creation. Remember, there are three personalities in one God (1 John 5:7)!

*"And God said; Let us make man in our own image . . ."* (Genesis 1: 26)

Job, the man who God blessed in his time, made a reference to the Holy Spirit concerning the creation of man.

*"The Spirit of God hath made me, and the breath of the Almighty hath given me life"* (Job 33: 4)

He knows all about you, your mission or purpose, where and how you can succeed in life. So, why not intermeddle with Him?

2.  He is the chief ambassador of God's kingdom on earth, who is qualified to show you your assignment on earth. He is the only one that knows the mind of God and the plans of God concerning us as Apostle Paul spoke about him.

*"But as it is written, Eye hath not seen, nor ear heard, neither have entered into the heart of man, things which God hath prepared for them that love him. But God hath revealed them unto us by his Spirit; for the Spirit searcheth all things, yea the deep things of God. For what man knoweth the things of man save the Spirit of man which is in him? Even so the things of God knoweth no man, but the Spirit of God"* (I Corinthians 2:9-11)

Jesus talked about his coming and his mission.

27

*"Howbeit when he, the Spirit of truth, is come, he will guide you into all truth about your life: for he shall not speak of himself; but whatsoever he shall hear, that shall he speak: and he will show you things to come, even your future"*(John 16:13, paraphrased)

3. He will show you your assignment phase by phase.

Your whole life is like a book documented by one man. You will only know it as God opens it up to you, by his Spirit page by page. All you need to do is to have contact with him.

4. Bishop David O. Oyedepo of Living Faith Church residing in Lagos, Nigeria, said that every authenticated proven commission is traceable to divine provision. But I add to it that it will take the Holy Spirit for you to know, through the eyes of Scriptures, the things (provision) that have been given to you for the success of your divine purpose.

*"Now we have received, not the spirit of the world, but the Spirit which is of God; that we might know the things that are freely given to us of God"* (1 Corinthians 2:12)

5. He will separate and bring other workers, who are like-minded to help you, as in the case of Paul.

*"As they ministered to the Lord, and fasted, the Holy Ghost said, Separate me Barnabas and Saul for the work whereunto I have called them"* (Acts 13:2)

Paul received the call alone from Jesus on his way to Damascus, but the Holy Spirit assigned Barnabas to him for effectiveness. He will do the same for you!

He directs you on where to go, what to do, and how to go about it. He will show you the path to tread on as in the case of Paul the apostle.

*"Now when they had gone throughout Phrygian and the region of Galatians, and were forbidden of the Holy Ghost to preach the word in Asia, after they were come to Mysia, they assayed to go into Bithynia: but the Spirit suffered them not. And they passing by Mysia came down to Troas. And a*

*vision appeared to Paul in the night; there stood a man of Macedonia, and prayed him, saying, Come over into Macedonia, and help us. And after he had seen the vision, immediately we endeavoured to go into Macedonia, assuredly gathering that the Lord called us for to preach the gospel unto them"* (Acts 16:6-10)

My prayer for you right now is for you to be able to understand the leadings of the Holy Spirit in your life.

When Jesus was filled with the Holy Ghost in river Jordan, the Holy Spirit made him know that the first thing he should do is to go into fasting and prayer. So he led him into the wilderness. If not, Jesus would have made the mistake of going into the city to preach, which was not the first thing for him. But thank God he was sensitive enough to the Holy Spirit.

The Holy Spirit is your boss. He is to take the major decision in your purpose. I have gone to places he never wanted me to go, done certain things he never wanted, and taken decisions against his own plan for my life and destiny. Until I repented from those erroneous steps, my life was peaceless, confused and frustrated. And I also lacked his full presence and provision.

Let me enumerate the things that depict his leading:

1. The feeling of his presence (Psalm 16: 11)
2. Peace (Isaiah 48:17, 18)
3. Joy (Psalm 16:11)
4. Acceptance (Ezekiel 3:6b)
5. Anointing (Acts 10:38)
6. Provision (Acts 28:10)
7. Proofs of signs and wonders (Mark 16:20)
8. Absolute protection (Psalm 23:5, Isaiah 63:9)
9. Daily fulfillment, and
10. Success in anything you do

When these things are not there with you, especially when you no longer have confidence whenever you meet with opposition, know that he is not with you.

*"For God has not given us the spirit of fear; but of power . . . and of a sound mind"* (2 Timothy 1:7)

Let us continue with why you must walk with Holy Spirit in your life:

7.  From time to time, the Holy Spirit lectures you concerning the work he has put in your hand.

*"But the anointing which ye receive of him abideth in you, and ye need not that any man teach you: but as the same anointing teacheth you of all things, and is truth, and is no lie, and even as it hath taught you, ye shall abide in him"* (1 John 2:27)

He is both your teacher and your reminder of the things that he has taught you. Good to hear that, Right?

*"But the comforter which is the Holy Ghost, who the Father shall send in my name, he shall teach you all things, and bring to your remembrance, whatsoever I have said unto you"* (John 14:26)

He gives you wisdom, spiritual knowledge and divine understanding of what he has sent you to do here on earth. He also produces the fear of God in you, and helps you to obey God in everything he instructs you to do as in the case of Jesus.

*"And the Spirit of the Lord shall rest upon him, the spirit of wisdom, and understanding . . . the spirit of knowledge and of the fear of the Lord"* (Isaiah 11:2)

*"And I will put my Spirit within you, and cause you to walk in my instructions which I shall tell you daily"* (Ezekiel 36: 27, Paraphrased)

He will always lead you excellently in everything, if you follow his instructions and seek his counsels daily and diligently, because he is the Spirit of excellence.

*"Then this Daniel was preferred above the presidents and princes, because an excellent spirit was in Him . . ."* (Daniel 6:3)

He keeps you from being destroyed.

*"Who are kept by the power of God through faith unto salvation . . ."* (1 Peter 1:5)

He is the person behind all the miraculous that will ever happen in your assignment (Romans 15:19). So he is your enabler and helper in all things. To be a comforter is to be a helper. You need him in your life and purpose. Without him, you can do nothing.

*". . . Not by might, nor by power, but by my Spirit, saith the Lord of hosts"* (Zechariah 4:6)

So link yourself to him now if you really want to see success in your life and purpose.

## THINGS THAT ANNOY THE HOLY SPIRIT

1.  Having no regard for him and his presence. When this happens, he withdraws his presence from your life. And this will make you totally confused and spiritually blinded. It has happened to me several times in the past. He comes into your life noticed but withdraws unnoticed. So be careful!
2.  Speaking corrupt words (Ephesians 4:29)
3.  Walking with sinners as close friends (1Corinthians 6:14-17)
4.  Lying (Psalm 101:7).
5.  Disobedience to his daily instructions without minding his feelings (1 Samuel 16:14)
6.  Slandering (Psalm 101:3-6)
7.  Immorality (1Corinthians 3:15-19)

If you really want to live in God's presence all the days of your life, desist from these things. I decree that the grace to live and stay in his presence come on you now in Jesus name!

### What Are The Things That Please Him?

1.  Purity (Isaiah 59:1, 2)
2.  Faith (Hebrews 11:6)
3.  Praises (Psalm 22:3; 147:1)
4.  Complete obedience to his instructions daily

5.  Communicating with God daily by studying and praying (Mark 1:35; 6:46)
6.  Respect for his person

All these Jesus practiced, and God was always with him.

*"Then said Jesus unto them, I do nothing of myself; but as my Father hath taught me, I speak these things. And he that sent me is with me: the Father hath not left me alone; for I do always those things that please Him"* (John 8:28, 29)

For this reason, he went about doing good and healing all that were oppressed of the devil; for God was with him (Acts 10: 38).

Therefore, walk in his steps and be a good follower of our Lord Jesus Christ. God will not leave you alone in Jesus' precious name!

# CHAPTER THREE

## HOW TO KNOW YOUR DESTINY

DESTINY IS SPIRITUAL. A carnal man cannot understand destiny because, God who created destiny does not relate to carnal mind, for it is in enmity with God. (Romans 8: 7). Therefore, it is impossible for a natural man to understand spiritual things, for they are spiritually discerned. It takes spiritual understanding to know the things that are of God. Destiny is a hidden treasure that demands its findings by any human, who cares to know his or her destiny.

*"It is the glory of God to conceal a thing: but the honour of kings is to search out a matter"* (Proverbs 25:2)

*"Man's goings is of the Lord; how can a man then understand his own way"* (Proverbs 20:24)

We are in the world of discovery. The greatest discovery in life is the discovery of one's destiny. Discovering your destiny is more precious than discovering gold. To discover your destiny is to find out what your life entails or to know the details of your life. More honorable is a man who searched out matters concerning his life than those that search for gold.

The Bible says, *"Man that is in honour, and understandeth not, is like the beasts that perish"* (Psalm 49:20).

Every destiny is honorable; but it is a pity if you don't know your placement in life. The hardest work so far in life is to be able to locate your place where you belong here on earth. The fingers are placed in the hands; the toes are placed on the legs; the nose is placed in the head. Locate your placement in life.

*". . . and they shall march every one on his ways, and they shall not break their ranks . . . they shall walk every one on his path"* (Joel 2:7b, 8b)

You have a placement on earth. You are not a spectator, but a partaker. Your service(s) is needed by your generation. So stop folding your hands watching others performing reasonably or rendering acceptable services. You may be an inventor, innovator or inventor's helper.

The following biblical examples of the people that got a revelation of their destinies in the next sub-topic will throw more light on your mental eyes to help you know that you are not a biological accident here on earth.

## YOU ARE BORN FOR AN ASSIGNMENT

The Bible is full of the histories of those who made life easy for others to climb. They were people of destinies, ranging from Genesis to Revelation:

1.   Adam: he was a keeper of the Garden of Eden.

*"And the Lord God planted a garden eastward in Eden; and there he put the man whom he had formed. And the Lord God took the man, and put him into the Garden of Eden to dress it and to keep it"* (Genesis 2:8, 15)

And through Adam, every living creature has a name.

*"And out of the ground the Lord God formed every beast of the field and every fowl of the air; and brought them unto Adam to see what he would call them: and whatever Adam called every living creature that was the name thereof"* (Genesis 2:19)

2.   Noah: through him, the destinies of generations were preserved from the floods, which made man to still exist on planet earth

today through the ark which he made. And through him, the curse that God placed upon the earth was lifted.

*"And Lamech lived an hundred eighty and two years, and begat a son: and he called his name Noah, saying, This same shall comfort us concerning our work and toil of our hands, because of the ground which the Lord hath cursed"* (Genesis 5:28, 29)

*"And Noah builded altar unto the lord; and took of every clean beast, and of every clean fowl, and offered burnt offerings on the altar. And the Lord smelled a sweet savior; and the Lord said in his heart; I will not again curse the ground any more for man's sake . . . While the earth remaineth, seed time and harvest . . . shall not cease"* (Genesis 8: 20-22)

3. Abraham: through him, the covenant between God and man was ushered into this world for you and me

*"And I will make of thee a great nation and I will bless thee, and make thy name great; and thou shalt be a blessing: and I will bless them that bless thee, and curse him that curseth thee: and in thee shall all the families of the earth be blessed"* (Genesis 12: 2, 3)

This same promise was fulfilled in Christ Jesus, and he that intermeddles with him or comes to him will become a partaker of these covenant promises of the bible.

*"Wherefore remember that ye being in time past Gentiles in the flesh, that at that time ye were without Christ, being aliens from the commonwealth of Israel, and strangers from, the covenants of promise, having no hope, and without God in the world: but now in Christ Jesus ye who some time were far off are made nigh by the blood of Christ. For he is our peace, who hath made both one, and hath broken down the middle wall of partition between us; having abolished in his flesh the enmity . . . and that he might reconcile both unto God in one body the cross, having slain the enmity thereby. For through him, we both have access by one Spirit unto the Father. Now therefore ye are no more strangers and foreigners, but fellow-citizens with the saints, and of the household of God"* (Ephesians 2: 11-16, 18 19)

*"That the blessing of Abraham might come on the gentiles through Jesus Christ; that we might receive the promise of the Spirit through faith"* (Galatians 3:14)

4. Jacob: he gave birth to the twelve tribes of Israel; and through him, Joseph was born, by whom the prophecy of God to Abraham about the slavery of the Israelites in a strange land came to pass.

*"And he said unto Abram, Know of a surety that thy seed shall be a stranger in a land that is not theirs, and shall serve them; and they shall afflict them four hundred years"* (Genesis15: 13)

This prophecy came to pass when all the sons of Jacob went to sojourn in Egypt through Joseph, when he was a Prime Minister in that same Egypt. After his death and the death of Pharaoh that was on sit in his time, the Israelites entered into their season of affliction as revealed by God to Abram.

*"Now there arose up a new king over Egypt, which knew not Joseph. And he said unto his people, behold, the people of Israel are more and mightier than we. Come on, let us deal wisely with them . . . Therefore they did set task masters to afflict them with their burdens"* (Exodus 1: 8-10)

This was the fulfillment of God's word to Abraham.

5. Joseph: he saved his people from unforeseen famine by the hand of God.

*"Moreover he called for a famine upon the land: he broke the whole staff of bread. He sent a man before them, even Joseph, who was sold for a servant: whose feet they hurt with fetters: he was laid in iron: the king sent and loosed him . . . He made him lord of his house, and ruler of all his substance"* (Psalm 105: 16-18, 20-21)

To his brethren, he said,

*"Now therefore be not grieved, nor angry with yourselves, that ye sold me hither: for God did send me before you to preserve life. For these two years hath the famine been in the land: and yet there are five years, in the which there shall neither be earning nor harvest. And God sent me before you*

*to preserve you a posterity in the earth, and to save your lives by a great deliverance"* (Genesis 45:5-7)

If not for Joseph, where would Israel be today? I believe that God also, has sent you to your generation at this time for a purpose, just as he sent Noah to preserve the lives of oncoming generations from the flood with the ark. There is a purpose for your life, don't waste it. Find it out, and go for it.

6.  Moses: through him, God delivered Israel from their bondage in Egypt and set them on their journey to Canaan.

*"He sent Moses his servant; and Aaron whom he had chosen. They shew his signs among them, and wonders in the land of Ham, he brought them forth also with silver and gold: and there was not one feeble person among their tribes. Egypt was glad when they departed: for the fear of them fell on them"* (Psalm 105:26, 27, 37-38)

God specially designed Moses for this common purpose. And when the time fully came, He called him by the sign of a burning bush. You can find this story in Exodus 2:24, 25; 3:1-10.

7.  Joshua: he was chosen to divide the land of Canaan portion by portion to the different tribes of Israel.

*"Now after the death of Moses the servant of the Lord it came to pass, that the Lord spake unto Joshua the son of Nun, Moses' minister, saying, Moses my servant is dead; now therefore arise, go over this Jordan, thou, and all this people unto the land which I do give to them, even to the children of Israel. Be strong and of a good courage: for unto this people shalt thou divide for an inheritance the land, which I sware unto their fathers to give them"* (Joshua 1:1, 2, 6)

This was his divine mission. I pray that God will show you your divine mission on earth too!

8.  Gideon: he was used of God to deliver the Israelites from the siege of the Midianites.

*"And there came an angel of the Lord, and sat under an oak which was in ophrah, that pertained unto Joash the Abiezrite: and his son Gideon threshed wheat by the wine press, to hide it from the Midianites, and the angel of the Lord appeared unto him, and said unto him, The Lord is with thee, thou mighty man of valour"* (Judges 6:11, 12)

When Gideon began to complain, the bible says, *"And the Lord looked upon him, and said, Go in this thy might, and thou shalt save Israel from the hand of the Midianites: have not I sent thee"* (vs. 14).

When he laid another complaint again in verse fifteen, the bible says, *"And the Lord said unto him, Surely I will be with thee, and thou shalt smite the Midianites as one man"* (vs. 16).

Then, after the victory, see what the Israelites said to him: *"The children of Israel said to Gideon, Rule thou over us, both thou and thy son, and thy son's son also: for thou hast delivered us from the hands of the Midianites"* (Judges 8: 22).

He sincerely fulfilled his destiny by the power of God. Can you see that his purpose brought him to the throne? That is the same way you will make it to the top—the place of affluence!

But listen; what is the predicament you were born to save your generation from? Look at that of Gideon: *"Thus was Midian subdued before the children of Israel, so that they lifted up their heads no more. And the country was in quietness forty years in the days of Gideon"* (Judges 8: 28).

What is that dream God has put in your mind concerning your country or society? Arise and take upon you the mandate and step into your destiny that has been before the world began (2 Timothy 1:9).

The Bible says, *"For whom he did foreknow, he also did predestinate . . . Whom he did predestinate, them he also called: and whom he called, them he also justified: and whom he justified, them he also glorified"* (Romans 8:29a, 30).

So, there are biblical proofs that you have been called into a destiny, which you have been already justified and glorified for. Wake up, and enter into your glory in Jesus name!

9. Saul: through him, the Israelites were ushered into the era of kingship, beginning with himself (1 Samuel 8: 1-5; 9:15-17).

10. Samuel: he was the first person that began the school of the prophets, which, at this time, is called **'Bible School'** or **'Bible Institute'.**

*"And it was told Saul, saying, Behold, David is at Naioth in Ramah. And Saul sent messengers to take David: and when they saw the company of the prophets prophesying, and Samuel standing as appointed over them . . ."* (1 Samuel 19:19-20)

The following statement is a confirmation from Dake's Annotated Reference Bible: "From this assembly of the prophets we got the idea of the school of the prophets. It seems that men who desired to be prophets gathered together to learn the ways of God and to be trained in divine matters. No doubt they sought God and were anointed with the Holy Spirit as in other periods. Certain men in every age have been spiritually minded and hungry for the Lord. There were such gatherings from Samuel's day on."

So Samuel was the first founder of spiritual institution called **'The School of The Prophets'.**

The prophets were the divine philosophers, the instructors, and the guides of the Hebrews in piety and virtue. They generally were retired people, seen in public mainly when they had some message of God to deliver. Their habitations and mode of life were plain, simple, and consistent.

Sons of the prophets were pupils of the prophets being trained in religion and habits of devotion and piety. They were not a monastic order but a group of theological students studying the Law and history of God's people, together with sacred poetry and music.

There were several schools of the prophets from the days of Samuel to the New Testament times, since Israel became a nation. Elisha was also a head of one of such schools in his time (2 Kings 4:1; 38; 5:22; 6:1-7; 9:1); but all these began with Samuel.

11. David: he was a shepherd boy, who God chose after his own heart to be the king of Israel, and whose beginning was rough; but his end was mighty. He was given a two-fold assignment.

Firstly, to be King over Israel; *"He chose David also his servant, and took him from the sheepfolds; from following the ewes, great with young he brought him to feed Jacob his people, and Israel his inheritance. So he fed them according to the integrity of his heart; and guided them by the skillfulness of his hands"* (Psalm 78:70-72; 2 Samuel 5:1-2).

Secondly, to save Israel from the hand of the philistines and all their enemies surrounding them; *"And Abner had communication with elders of Israel, saying, Ye sought for David in times past to be king over you: now then do it: for the Lord hath spoken of David, saying, By the hand of my servant David I will save my people Israel out of the hand of the Philistines, and out of the hand of all their enemies"* (2 Samuel 3:17, 18).

He was also the one whom God gave the pattern of his temple through the inspiration of the Holy Spirit, but was not allowed to build it.

*"Then David gave to Solomon his son the pattern of the porch, and of the houses thereof, and of the inner parlour thereof, and of the place of the mercy seat, and the pattern of all that he had by the Spirit, of the court of the house of the Lord, and of all the house of the Lord, and of all the chambers round about, of the treasuries of the house of God, and of the treasuries of the dedicated things: this, said David, The Lord made me understand in writing by his hand upon me, even all the works of this pattern"* (1 Chronicles 28:11, 12, 19)

12. Solomon: this man was created purposely for the building of God's temple. See what his father, David, said to him, *"Take heed now; for the Lord hath chosen thee to build an house for the sanctuary: be strong and do it"* (1 Chronicles 28:10).

Now let us hear the testimony of Solomon himself: *"Now it was in the heart of David my father to build an house for the name of the Lord God of Israel. But the Lord said to David my father, Forasmuch as it was in thine heart to build an house for my name, thou didst well in that it was in thine heart: notwithstanding thou shall not build the house; but thy son which shall come forth out of thy loins, he shall build the house for my name. The Lord therefore hath performed his word that he hath spoken: for I am risen up in the room of David my father, and am set on the throne of Israel, as the Lord promised, and have built the house for the name of the Lord God of Israel"* (2 Chronicles 6:7-10).

What really happened between Solomon and his father, David, was what is called 'The crossed hands of God'. This same thing happened between Manasseh and Ephraim.

When Jacob was about to die, he called for Joseph. And Joseph, when coming, came with his two sons (Manasseh and Ephraim). He placed the eldest son, Manasseh, under Jacob's right hand; and Ephraim, the younger, under the left hand of Jacob his father, knowing fully well that his father was about to go the way of the dead. But according to destiny, his father Jacob, being in the Spirit, crossed his hands over each other and place his right hand on Ephraim and his left on Manasseh, and then began to bless them in Joseph's presence. When Joseph saw it, he was grieved, and he cautioned his father to change his hand. But thank God for his father, who the Spirit of God was upon.

Look at what Jacob said, *". . . I know it, my son, I know it: Manasseh also shall become a people, and he also shall be great: but truly, his younger brother shall be greater than he and his seed shall become a multitude of nation"* (Genesis 48:19).

And afterward, he blessed them according to their destiny, and set Ephraim before Manasseh as they go from his presence (Genesis 48:8-20).

Listen to me; no matter what your parents are doing to you, no matter the partiality they are playing in your home, no matter what your teachers or lecturers or managers are doing to you, your destiny abides forever, waiting to be manifested.

Let all of you out there stop struggling for what is not your destiny as David was to do concerning building the house of God. Find out your calling and stay stuck to it; for whatever God has made you to do, he will empower you to accomplish.

13. Jehu: under whose hand and in whose time, the word of God concerning Ahab and Jezebel came to pass (2 Kings 9, 10).

14. Prophet Isaiah: in this man's time, God revealed the birth and death of our Messiah—Jesus Christ (Isaiah 9:6, 7; 53:1-12). And the prophecy which he prophesied according to the revelation that God showed him brought great light, hope and joy to the nation Israel and the world at large (Isaiah 9:2; 60:1-3). I repeat, something is about to happen by your own hands!

15. Jesus: he took away the sins of the whole world. By his stripes, sicknesses and diseases were healed from the body of mankind. He put Satan to shame and brought us back to glory. He removed the enmity between our Father (God) and us. He ushered in grace and the Kingdom of God into the world. Through him, we became victorious over the world (1 Peter 1:24, 25; Ephesians 1:19-23; Hebrews2: 10, 14; Ephesians 2:16, 18; 1 John 5:4).

16. Paul the Apostle: he was an apostle of the gospel of Jesus to the Gentiles. Through him, the Gentiles received the gospel of the Lord Jesus.

*"But when it pleased God, who separated me from my mother's womb, and called me by his grace, to reveal his Son in me, that I might preach him among the heathen [Gentiles . . ."* (Galatians 1:15, 16)

*"For he that wrought effectually in Peter to the apostleship of the circumcision, the same was mighty in me toward the Gentiles"* (Galatians 2: 8)

Finally, through him also, 50% of the New Testament was written. In addition, the gospel of Jesus Christ was expanded to us through the grace of God that was on Paul's life.

17. John the Beloved: God through him made us to know the hidden things concerning the future (Eschatology).

*"The revelation of Jesus Christ, which God gave unto him, to shew unto his servants things which must shortly come to pass; and he sent and signified it by his angel unto his servant John: who bare record of the word of God, and of the testimony of Jesus Christ, and of all things that he saw"* (Revelation 1:1-2)

These are some of the names of those whom God used mightily in the bible days.

Time and space will not permit me to talk about people like Nelson Mandela of South Africa, Abraham Lincoln, Martin Luther Jr. and Kenneth E. Hagin of the United States of America, and so many others.

I like also to announce to you that you are not left out of God's program for this world. In every generation, there are pioneers and pioneers' helpers. It is either you are a leader or a subordinate to a leader in one area of life or the other. Please find out your placement in this world and be there.

Paul said, *"Brethren, let every man, wherein he is called, therein abide with God."* (1 Corinthians 7:24).

I see you succeeding in Jesus' precious name!

In chapter one, I talked about knowing your individuality and purpose for existence. If you have really read through it, it will interest you to know that comparing yourself to another is the beginning of failure in life.

I like you to avoid the act of comparison and value who you are. Even if the moon shines, the stars have their values.

*"For as we have many members in one body, and all members have not the same office: so we, being many, are one body in Christ, and every one members one of another"* (Romans 12:4-5)

*"If the whole body were an eye, where were the hearing? If the whole were hearing, where was the smelling? But now hath God set the members every one of them in the body, as it hath pleased him. And the eye cannot say unto the hand, I have no need of thee: nor again the head to the feet, I have*

*no need of you. Nay, much more those members of the body, which seem to be more feeble, are necessary: and those members of the body, which we think to be less honourable, upon these we bestow more abundant honour; and our uncomely parts have more abundant comeliness"* (1 Corinthians 12:17, 18, 21-23)

I want you to know that you are the one your generation is waiting for. Your death will mean much of a great loss to your generation. No matter how great a car manufacturer is, he still needs the service of a toothpick maker. Stop neglecting yourself; for you are highly needed. Wake up from your slumber. You are the light of the world and the salt of the earth. Don't die with those potentials hiding inside of you. No matter the pressure surrounding you, envision yourself already shining. No matter how dark your night season may seem to be, your day must surely break forth, because no matter how the night wages war against the sun, it is inevitable that the sun will emerge. You too will emerge!

In your generation, something good must happen through you. Your name must be recorded in the Guinness Book of Records. You will never pass away from this earth unnoticed! Your generation shall benefit your existence. Somebody will definitely say, **"Thank God that he was born in my time!"** When people will narrate the history of your society and country anywhere in this world, your name will be mentioned because of your impact on their lives! And so, for this reason, I adjure you; don't leave this world without the world being affected by the virtue(s) that you carry on your inside. You will make it. Hallelujah!

One thing I will never forget to tell you is this: many may not believe in you nor patronize what you carry on your inside; but nevertheless, those whom God has destined to benefit from what you are carrying will surely come for you (John 10:26-27).

As God's Prophet, I decree that everything that God has destined for you will surely come to pass in Jesus!

## HOW TO KNOW YOUR DESTINY

1. God reveals it (Jeremiah 33:3; John 16:13). It will take you to call on God for it.

2.  Through scriptural illumination (2 Peter 1:19). An encounter with God's word can reveal it to you.

3.  Through divine encounter (Mark 1:16, 17; Exodus 3:1-6; Genesis 12:1-3). Peter was a fisherman, when Jesus encountered him and introduced him into his true destiny. So, it will take you knowing Jesus, who is the Shepherd and the Bishop of your soul (1 Peter 2:25), in order for him to show you your purpose as he did to Peter and Paul (Acts 9:1-16). Remember, until Moses and Abraham encountered God, they never knew their purpose and destiny. I pray that God will show himself to you concerning your destiny in Jesus' mighty name!

4.  It comes through trance as you keep meditating on the realities of life. This is what we call 'Standing upon your watch' (Habakkuk 2:1-3; Numbers 24:16).

5.  It comes via night visions (Job 33:14-18).

6.  You can know it by looking inward. That is, looking within you.

**Why inward? a**. What do you think you can do best in your life that can prove your true color, making you a star? b. What does your soul loves to do, despite the stress in it? c. What is the thing that has a force of attraction toward you, or that attracts your interest when you see people doing it, or hear people talk about it? (As for me, nothing pleases me than the gospel work). d. What do you always envision with your mental eyes, either through night visions or trances that gives you inner joy? e. What do you think about that gives you peace, inner satisfaction and a settled mind? f. What you desperately hate, which attracts your concern, is a clue to what you are born to correct. g. In what do you have pleasure doing, even when you are not paid? h. What will you like to do if the whole world is ready to sponsor you? i. What will you like to do, no matter the discouragement around you? That is what you are created and anointed for. Go for it!

As you discover your assignment in life, I joined the stars of heaven to welcome you to the world of success in Jesus' name!

# CHAPTER FOUR

## THE POWER OF THE MIND

### (A) MIND DYNAMICS

In everyone's life, the subject of the mind is never to be neglected. Destiny cannot be attained, except by a divine instrument called "Mind". The mind is the drawing board for your future. The journey of life begins in the mind. Your mind is the pivot around which your whole life revolves. It determines your direction in life. That is why the Bible tells us in Proverbs 4:23, saying, *"Keep thy heart with all diligence; for out of it are the issues of life"* (Proverbs 4:23).

The mind is the place where future images are formed, and you see them as mental pictures through vision—insight. What you cannot envision, you cannot achieve; and you cannot pursue what you have not seen because, no man chases the unknown. What you see is what motivates your action in life.

The mind is the centre of man's life. As compass and direction are to the ship in the midst of the sea, so your mind is the only eyes your spirit has. If it is blinded, it is over for you except the Holy Spirit heals you.

The mind is the spiritual satellite of the body with which you capture divine purpose and future through revelation.

Whatever enters the mind has power to be transmuted into its physical counterpart. So every man's life is the product of his mind. Your attitude reveals the thoughts that take place in your mind. Whatever you see or hear, you are bound to think on; and whatever you think, you feel; and whatever you feel, you are bound to do one day.

The mind and the members of your body are interwoven. The attitude that finds its expression through humans is a product that begins its journey in the mind. You can't stop what you do until you stop what you think upon. When the temperature of a thought in your mind has attained its full stage or boiling point, it has no option than to evaporate out of you through your character. So the mind has power to govern your destiny. Vision of one's purpose takes place in the mind. If your mind is powerfully negative or positive, your life will be either also (Matthew 12:35, 33).

Change begins in the mind. Whatever occupies your mind has power to occupy your life also. So if you want to change your life, change what begins as a seed in your mind!

Anything you meditate upon for a long time produces the passion for its pursuit. So keep your mind busy by thinking only on positive things and on what God has shown to you about your future; and do not fail to think on God's promises in the Bible about your destiny.

*". . . Whatever is true, whatever is worthy of reverence and is honourable and seemly, whatever is just, whatever is pure, whatever is lovely and lovable, whatever is kind and winsome and gracious, if there is any virtue and excellence, if there is anything worthy of praise, think on and weigh and take account of these things [fix your minds on them]* (Philippians 4:8, AMP)

The images formed in your mind must definitely come to pass in your life. It is the principle of the mind. Be careful of what your eyes see or what you hear daily in your life! Remember, your destiny is tied to your mind; so guard it jealously.

The Bible says, *"He that hath no rule over his own spirit is like a city that is broken down, and without walls"* (Proverbs 25:28).

## The tenets of the mind

1. You are equal to your mindset.
2. Your rating in life is determined by the quality of your mind.
3. Excellence or mediocrity is determined by the level of your personal development or mental exposure.
4. Exposure is gotten through reading, traveling, research and positive social indulgences and relationship.
5. Intelligence is the ability to apply the product of your exposure correctly.
6. Mind power is in high demand; both in leadership, economic and industrial communities. It is the most valuable product in the world of success and excellence today. It is a scarcely commodity.
7. Exposure generates understanding, while understanding is the bucket you can use to draw ideas from the well of wisdom (Proverbs 20:5). Remember, the mind is the sit of wisdom.
8. Creativity, which gives birth to invention and innovation, is the master key in the world of success. The creative and innovative people use the non-creative and non-innovative people to achieve their aims. Creativity is a function of the mind.
9. Deep thinking, which is the function of diligence—hard work, gives birth to creativity. Creative people rule the world. Those who can think have the ability to change or rule the world; they have ability to handle situations. Life does not order them around, they just take charge.
10. Mind power provides the ladder with which to climb out of the pit of obscurity and mediocrity.
11. Those who can alter the mode of life around them are great thinkers. Exacting on the divine deposits of the mind is not an easy task; it takes time, brain energy, discipline, courage; and sometimes, it involves thinking companion(s), either human resources (people you can see), or material resources (books, tapes, CDs, periodicals, internet, and the environment that can provide you the necessary information you need; and don't forget, it takes money to access these informative materials and also to travel to places of your demand.
12. The best part of you is hidden deep within your inner man; only mental exposure can bring it out. Determine to fight for it!

**Note:** Remember, those who love pleasure cannot leave their comfort zone; and they are only found beneath the mountains of life. Sacrifice is what it takes to be on top. Do it for yourself!

Don't forget, gain is the product of pain; so be aggressive to pay the price for excellence. Its benefit cannot be compared to the labor involved. You can make it happen!

## VISION: A COVENANT FORCE FOR SUCCESS

The Dictionary definition of **'Vision'** states that:

1.   Vision is the power of seeing or imagining, looking ahead, grasping the truth that underlines a fact. It is the unfolding of all that can be seen from a certain point.

2.   Vision is something seen especially by the mind's eyes or the power of imagination, or something seen during sleep or in a trance-like state; for example, to have a vision of great wealth and success.

The Biblical definition of **'Vision'** states that it is the unfolding of God's plan and purpose for your life.

A wise man said that vision is the internalized mental picture of an enviable future.

In Jeremiah 29:11, God says,

*"For I know the thought that I think towards you, saith the Lord, thoughts of peace, and not of evil, to give you an expected end."*

NIV translation puts it this way: **". . . To give you a hope and a future."**

As I have said in one of the previous chapters that God is the only one that has the ability to show you what your future and life entail, He will definitely show it to you through vision.

As defined previously, success is the step-by-step achievement of a divine purpose. This is absolutely impossible without the role of vision.

Until you see the future of what you are born to do and to be, you will never be sure you will succeed.

Assurance delivers you from doubt and waver. It eradicates instability from your life. It prevents you from a life of trial and error—a frustrating method of living.

Vision produces a strong faith in you, knowing that God will always bring his word to pass in your life.

## THE DIFFERENCES BETWEEN A DIVINE VISION AND A HUMAN AMBITION

| DIVINE VISION | HUMAN AMBITION |
|---|---|
| It is clear and precise. | It is shabby and, sometimes, undefined. |
| It impacts faith. | It is always full of doubts. |
| It is pursued by grace. | It is pursued by struggle. |
| It commands followers because of its clarity. | It tires everyone that follows it, because it confuses. |
| It commands divine favor and backing. | It is full of human tricks and commands no divine backing. |
| It is linear because it is achieved step by step with the end in view. | It is frustrating because its end is not known, and it is zigzag in nature. |
| It is a vector quantity because it has direction. God leads you through in it. | It is a scalar quantity because it has no direction, and does not enjoy divine leading because it is usually contrary to God's plan for your life. |
| It breaks the yoke of hardship and struggle in your life. | It generates hardship because of human struggle that acquaints it. |

| It gives hope and creates the spirit of persistence in you. | Oppositions frustrate it because, the assurance of its possible dividends is not certain. |
| --- | --- |
| 10 It motivates you into action because God tells you from time to time how to go about it. | It is entangled with slothfulness because it does not have an assurance of its future success. |

## THE POWER OF VISION

*"Where there is no vision, the people perish"* (Proverbs 29:18a)

Sometimes in your life, it will be as if you should no longer go forward because of discouragement; but I assure you that if truly what you are pursuing is a divine vision from God, definitely, it has a future, and the end must surely come true.

Let me ask you a question: what do you think that kept Joseph going in life, even when the road he plied did not seem to be what God revealed to him? What do you think made Moses and Joshua persist, even when enemies that seemed to be greater, more numerous and mightier than they were attacked them in their journey to Canaan? It is because God spoke to them. And for every godly vision, there is a divine backing. This is what vision can do in one's life.

Vision breaks the yoke of hardship, especially in times of famine.

Let's look at the case of Isaac: *"And there was a famine in the land beside the first famine that was in the days of Abraham. And Isaac went unto Abimelech king of the Philistines unto Gerar. And the Lord appeared unto him, and said, Go not down into Egypt; dwell in the land which I shall tell thee of; sojourn in this land, I will be with thee, and will bless thee . . . Then Isaac sowed in that land, and received in the same year an hundredfold: and the Lord blessed him. And the man waxed great, and went forward and grew until he became very great; for he had possession of flocks and possession of herds, and great store of servants; and the Philistines envied him"* (Gen. 26: 1-3, 12-14).

When everyone was striving for what to make a living with, a man of vision, that God appeared to, and instructed on what to do, was busy making riches. When God gives you a vision of what to do, hardship becomes a thing of the past. Vision is a 'mocker' of difficulties. It shows you the way out of problems; it is like a torch light in the midst of obscurity. It is called divine knowledge or light from heaven. Even in the midst of your present difficulty, you need an encounter with God, who should tell you what to do in order to get out of that mess. I pray that a light from heaven shines on your path right now in the name of Jesus!

I don't know what you may be passing through now, but may I let you know that if you can receive light from heaven right now, you can triumphantly walk out of it without stress.

Let me let you know also that in time of hardship, the best prayer to pray is the prayer of enquiry—finding out what, where and how to go about things in order to bring a change.

I see your joy overflow right now. I hear songs of melody springing out of your innermost part from today. I see you becoming a problem solver and not a quitter. I see you becoming an inventor from today. Your world will soon begin to look for you. Your house will soon begin to overflow with pleasant things. I decree that, by the virtue of what you are just learning from this book, may you become a co-creator with God in the name of Jesus. This year all that you have been looking for will run after you. All your complaints and murmurings against God in your past days have come to an end today. The hell of life that opened its mouth against your destiny will be closed as you receive a dynamic vision for your life. All your confusion has come to an end right now. Many of those that mocked you will soon become your employees through God's mercy as you locate a vision this year. Testimony shall never end in your life, beginning from now!

I see you becoming the head of your department, where you are working because of divine ideas from heaven. You will make it. Your confusion has come to an end. Many who laughed at you before will bow to you this year in Jesus' precious name!

It could be that for many years you have been humiliated by financial predicament due to lack of qualitative idea(s), but this year it will become your subject. You will have dominion over money. Many who you begged from yesterday will soon be depending on you. They will come to you this year crawling for help. Your family's disgrace has come to an end forever. Laughter has become your portion from now. Praise the Lord!

A man of vision never dies in the fire of life nor capsizes in the sea of life. No matter how difficult life is to him, vision will make a persistent fellow out of him, just as in the case of Jesus.

*". . . Who for the joy that was set before Him endured the cross, despising the shame . . ."* (Hebrews 12: 2B)

The vision of your future produces strength in you, and makes you go against the obstacles of life that are before you. It shows you your path to financial buoyancy. It makes you to be proud of life, no matter the circumstances you are passing through.

Without an idea in the mind, the slothfulness of the hand is inevitable. It is vision that uncovers an idea to your mind. Vision removes fear from your eyes and gives you confidence.

David, when he saw how honor and dignity, riches and glory, even kingship position, which he had been anointed for would come to him after he must have killed Goliath, moved forward without the fear of death against the giant and brought him down. This is what divine vision can do.

Vision provides reason for living. A man of vision sees life as a divine opportunity. This makes him handle such opportunity positively.

## PSEUDO VISION ANALYSIS

There are many things that look like vision but they are not vision themselves. These kinds of things are called **'pseudo vision'**.

The word 'pseudo' means 'false'. So, what are pseudo-visions?

1.  Ambition: it is not vision. This is creating your plan without God's instruction or revelation. Vision is God-made, while ambition is man-made.
2.  Impression: being carried away with what you see in someone's life.
3.  Human imagination: this is forming your own mental picture(s) that does not have God's approval on them.
4.  Situation: what someone is passing through at a particular time can lead him to do a thing that God didn't plan for him or her, e.g. work, business, ministry, etc.
5.  Reaction: this is breaking away from others to form your personal business or any other thing without God's approval. Its major cause is financial contention or pride.
6.  People's confirmation: being carried away by what people call you or say about you.

## HOW DOES VISION COME?

Vision is not a dream that comes by the multitude of businesses. As I have earlier said, the bible defines it as an insight into God's plan: the unfolding of God's program to an individual, incorporating the specific area of assignment in which the individual is elected or chosen to function. It is having a supernatural insight into one's placement in life. It is a spiritual language by which God transmits his plan to his chosen vessel. It can be transmitted through the following:

1.  Godly night dreams

*"For God speaketh once, yea twice, yet man perceiveth it not: in a dream, in a vision of the night, when deep sleep falleth upon men, in slumbering upon the bed"* (Job 33: 14, 15)

2.  Studying God's word

*"We have also a more sure word of prophecy; whereunto ye do well that ye take heed, as unto a light that shineth in a dark place, until the day dawn, and the day star arise in your hearts"* (2 Peter 1:19)

Studying God's word causes an illumination in your mental eyes. When the mind is without understanding, it is dark. But when knowledge comes, it is like a light that shines in a dark place—your mind, causing an illumination. This is called "Understanding". It is a divine medium that God uses to show people who they really are.

The Psalmist says,

*"The entrance of thy words giveth light; it giveth understanding to the simple"* (Psalm 119:130)

This is an assurance that God speaks to us through his word concerning our destinies.

3.  Paying attention to the Holy Spirit

*"Howbeit when he, the Spirit of truth is come, he will guide you into all truth . . . And he will shew you things to come"* (John 16:13)

4.  Seeking the Lord in prayer and calling on him

*"Call unto me, and I will answer thee, and shew thee great and mighty things, which thou knowest not"* (Jeremiah 33:3)

5.  Divine imagination: when you separate yourself from noisy environments to a solitary place to think about your life, if God is with you and favors you, light will definitely come to your mind from heaven.

*"He hath said, which heard the words of God, and knew the knowledge of the most High, which saw the vision of the Almighty, falling into a trance, but having his eyes open"* (Numbers 24:16)

God speaks with pictures which appear before your mental eyes by insight through imagination. According to scientists, one mental picture is equal to about a thousand words precisely.

I pray that God would show you a vision by the end of today!

## THE ENEMIES OF VISION

If vision is truly the beginning of one's true life, which begins in the mind, it definitely would command our enemy's attention.

*"For a great door and effectual is opened unto me, and there are many adversaries"* (1 Corinthians 16:9)

But we have only one arch-enemy called the "devil" that goes about like a roaring lion, seeking for whom he may devour. The devil cannot master your life except he first of all blind your mind from God and from the vision of your true life.

*"In whom the god of this world hath blinded the minds of them . . ."* (2 Corinthians 4:4)

So the devil is the only mind blinder that the world has today.

**How does he blind the minds of men?**

1.  Through drunkenness: This is an unhealthy habit, which does not promote success. It drains the pocket and renders your mind inactive from having God's divine revelation of your purpose and future.

*"But they also have erred through wine, and through strong drink are out of the way; the priest and the prophet have erred through strong drink, they are swallowed up of wine, they are out of the way through strong drink; they err in vision, they stumble in judgment"* (Isaiah 28:7)

2.  Indiscriminate or premarital sex: Sex simply means **"let us bind ourselves together by blood agreement"**. So it is a game of blood between two persons. Remember, the life of any animal is in the blood (Genesis 9:4). So any time you are mating together sexually with an opposite sex, you are having an exchange of blood with each other. That is to say that you are pouring out your life to such a fellow with whom such game is played.

Talking about marital sex, it is known as covenant bonding after marriage, when it is done the first time. Its continuation is called covenant renewal. For this sake, whenever you have any sex with any opposite sex, you are entering into blood oath with the person; especially when promises are made before sexual intercourse. This is why premarital sex is dangerous. It involves tying your souls together. (Soul is another word for life). And being not declared as one, your families not being witnesses, you are committing fornication. And this is where the judgment of God comes. By this, you open your life to curses.

Moreover, as far as the two of you are individually apart (not being married), you are splitting your life to the other (when you have sex together), which causes divided mind or double soul. This makes you unfocused. Your attention will be divided in life.

The Spirit of life behind your vision will depart from you because your mind is polluted, thereby making your divine vision gone.

Remember, the Holy Spirit is the giver of vision, and the one who helps a man to bring his vision to fruition. When He is gone from your life, your destiny will be bleak. So be careful! (1Peter 2: 11; 1Kings 11: 1-4)

3.   The third thing that destroys vision is drug addiction. I don't know how true this is; but I read once from an article in year 2000 that N. B. C. news announced on the 16th of May 1998 that over 750,000 people die each year in the world due to nicotine addiction. U.S. Surgeon General C. Evereth Koop openly announced that nicotine addiction is more dangerous than cocaine or heroin. Remember, drug addiction destroys both physical and mental health. Drug disturbs the mind, which afterward negatively affects the whole system of man. You can't be smoking and have your mind healthy to receive or retain the vision of God for your life. Once your mind is destabilized, your vision is scattered.

I pray that you would be free from these habits in Jesus' name!

In conclusion, immoral lifestyle is deadly venom from the pit of hell. It is called 'Worldliness'. The Holy Spirit hates it. Read the following Scriptures: 1 John 2:15-17; James 4:4, 5.

# YOUR SUCCESS LIES IN YOUR HANDS

Oh yes, your success lies in your hands. Every man's life is tied to his will or choice, and every man's life is opened to negative and positive opportunities; and all these opportunities have their express road in the mind.

I like talking about the mind because this is the centre of a man's whole life. Every man's life revolves around his mind where thoughts or reasoning is exercised.

The Bible says, *"Keep thy heart with all diligence; for out of it are the issues of life"* (Proverbs 4:23).

Many in life take so many journeys into the negative world through their minds. In the spiritual realm, negative thoughts are 'persona non grata'. They don't wait for invitations. They come on their own, while positive thoughts are dug out of the very depth of the mind through rigorous meditation. It is the hardest work so far. We have two main personalities behind the two kinds of thought. The Spirit of God for the positive, while the negative is of Satan, our arch enemy.

As I was saying in one of the previous chapters, success begins in the mind by the snaps of mental pictures of great tomorrow. Satan knows about the principle and work of the mind, which is the greatest asset that God endowed us with on our inside. The devil knows that our life is a product of what we strongly believe in our heart.

*"For as he (man) thinketh in his heart, so is he . . ."* (Proverbs 23: 7a)

And the principle of faith states that **"As a man believes, let it be so unto him."**

You cannot change what is happening around you until you change what you strongly believe. When your belief has grown to its fullest, it has no option than to bear its fruits outward.

The mind has two parts: the conscious and the subconscious mind as I have earlier said. When a man receives an information for the first time and does not reject it; and if it is daily meditated upon and finally accepted, it will be transferred to his subconscious mind, where information is no longer subject to analysis, but only goes down to a man's emotional system, which afterward expresses itself on the outward. Remember, what you hear or see determines what you think, and what you think produces what you feel, which boils down to your actions either through words or deeds.

Now, in terms of success, whatever you don't fully believe, you will never run with nor pursue after in life. So, the devil knows about all this. For that, he goes about like a fallacious rumor bearer or informant, seeking for people that do not know their true person to give them fake news about themselves.

The Bible says, **"Let all men be liars and God be true."** It is only God that knows you really. Nobody else can fully tell about you except the manufacturer, who knows the quality of materials he has used on you physiologically, psychologically and spiritually. No negative circumstance happening around you, or any weakness within you, can truly tell who you are. Your worth and personality are tied to your strength, gifts, talent and ability. I am talking about your endowed divine potential(s), which is hidden within the earthen vessel called the body that you carry.

The Bible says, *"But the anointing which ye have received of him abideth in you, and ye need not that any man teach you: but as the same anointing teacheth you of all things, and is true, and is no lie, and even as it hath taught you, ye shall abide in him"* (1 John 2: 27).

Everyone is entitled to his/her opinion. So, don't let all that the devil tells you or all that people say about you negatively move you, except what can be corrected to your advantage. They are all lies. God is the only true one. Believe in God, and all that he tells you, either through godly or scripturally proven revelation (night vision or trance) or through the bible itself. If you have a wrong notion about yourself, you will act wrongly. So I suggest you tell yourself the truth from God's word. It is the only book that never lies in this whole universe.

# 13 POSITIVE SECRETS FOR FORMING A MENTAL SUCCESS IMAGE

1.  God shows you your strength, abilities, potential(s), and the future success you will achieve with them. So declare them.
2.  Satan shows you your weaknesses, emptiness, nothingness and your negative past or present. He paints a negative picture about you in your mind through your imagination. So what you do is to cast down all negative imaginations and every stronghold of belief, and bring into captivity every evil thought to the obedience of Christ. Then declare what God says about you (2 Corinthians 10: 3-5; Isaiah 43: 26).
3.  God's pictures about your future produce joy and peace. Satan's pictures produce sorrows. For this, give no room for negative thoughts.

Hear the instruction of Paul, the Apostle: *"Finally, brethren whatsoever things are true, whatsoever things are honest, whatsoever things are just, whatsoever things are pure, whatsoever things are of good report: if there be any virtue, and if there be any praise, think on these things"* (Philippians 4: 8).

I want to conclude this by saying that you should never let the devil lock you up in the prison of sorrow and depression.

4.  Inferiority complex, self-intimidation and low self-esteem that you ascribe to yourself are products of the belief you released to agree with the negative pictures about you that the devil showed you. So stop believing Satan. The Bible calls him the father of lies. A great man of God, Arch-Bishop Benson Idahosa (late) once said, "If you give the devil attention, he will give you direction."
5.  Only your manufacturer (God) knows you, and apart from him, nobody knows the complete truth about you. The content of your make-up is contained in a book, as your divine manual, called **"The Bible"**. Read it every day and night and discover your real self (James 1: 22-25).
6.  Everyone has a 100% attention to give to negative or positive mental images in his or her mind. The negative images are called demonic inspiration. I suggest that the whole percentage of

attention be given to the positive images God shows us through his manual—the bible. It tells us our divine make-up. Positive images are formed by divine inspiration through the Holy Spirit.

*"But there is a spirit in man: and the inspiration of the Almighty giveth them understanding"* (Job 32:8)

The measure of attention you give to godly information, by meditation, will determine how far you will go in the world of success, because positive information breeds success, while negative information breeds failure. God and Satan daily provide you with informative materials in picture form. It is your choice that produced what you are seeing physically in your life today. Be careful!

I reverse every evil operating in your life right now in Jesus' name!

7. What you believe you are is what you see yourself becoming. Your level of insight about you, either negative or positive, depends on the measure of attention you give to either Satan or God. So if you can give all your attention to God by listening to his word or studying his word, praise God!

8. The imagination you give attention to determines your direction and character.

9. God shows you your abundance; the devil shows you your lack. What you see mentally by insight determines what you pursue. Remember, no one pursues an abstract. This is why there is idleness, because of lack of divine vision. If the mind of a man is blinded toward his good future, the idleness of his hands is inevitable.

10. God believes in your future, and he shows you the future exploits you are to make, while the devil shows you your past failures and mistakes in order to depress your mind and make you regret your existence on earth.

11. Satan shows you why you are not fit to live, but God shows you why you must live. I therefore beckon to you to shift your boat of life from the waters of Satan and come close to God, who will never condemn you for any mistake you make but is ever ready to give you a chance again. In fact, know this, that God sometimes allows us to make certain mistakes because of our self-confidence

in order for us to see our self-insufficiency; but he will still uphold and mold our destinies (Psalm 37:23-24; 2 Chronicles 7: 14).

12. Satan with his negative information will make nobody out of you if you give him room to define you, but God will make somebody out of you with his word if only you can apply them to your life.

13. Lastly, it is God's truth about you that will set you free from the negative belief you have about yourself, which has been determining your negative, ungodly actions.

*"And you shall know the truth, and the truth shall set you free"* (John 8:32)

So, *"Fight the good fight of faith. Lay hold on positive information"* (1 Timothy 6:12, Paraphrased).

*"Above all, take the shield of faith with which you can quench the demonic manipulations of the devil on your mind"* (Ephesians 6:16, Paraphrased)

*"Put on the whole truth (armour) of God, that ye may be able to stand against the wiles of the devil"* (Ephesians 6:11, Paraphrased)

God bless you!

# CHAPTER FIVE

## YOU ARE TOO LOADED TO FAIL.

FAILURE BEGINS IN LIFE when you begin to ply the road you are not born for. It is ridiculous for an airplane to fly on the ground or for a ship to sail on the land or a car to run in the air or on the sea. You have a divine fashion. Every man's worth is tied to his ability. There is something God has laid on your inside that makes you a tool in God's hand for the service of your generation's need. This thing is called **'Talent'**. When this talent is discovered, which calls for individual uniqueness, and developed, it can make you a celebrity in the world; and it can also make you to be in high demand to your generation, especially to those who are in need of such service that you carry and are able to discern your product as a solution to their problem(s).

## A. THE DYNAMICS OF TALENT

In 1998 God revealed **Ephesians 1:18** to me in a different way.

"The eyes of your understanding being enlightened; that ye may know what is the hope of your calling and what is the riches of the glory of his inheritance in the saints."

I see this inheritance as a hidden potential that God endowed us with. It is expedient that you see the glory of what you are carrying on your inside, and the riches contained in it.

The Bible says. *"In whom also we have obtained an inheritance, being predestinated according to the purpose of him who worketh all things after the counsel of his own will"* (Ephesians 1:11).

This inheritance also, by my understanding, is to be used to expand God's Kingdom and to solve human problems, not only on the spiritual side but also on the physical side.

This inheritance can be called **"ability"** or **"talent"**. When I talk about **"talent",** I am talking about something that determines your calling. For example, the problem of light, wears, mobility and other scientific and technological problems have been solved by people who God sent to this earth to help us as they discovered their destinies. Thank God for sending them to bridge these gaps of life.

In Exodus 31, 35, 36, certain people had creative abilities in them by virtue of the Holy Spirit indwelling in them, and they began to manufacture things meant for the tabernacle and the priests, even for the high priest.

What is talent? Talent is like a colorful flower that attracts birds toward you to sing joy to your heart. It is the bedrock of your enjoyment in life. Talent, when traded, is the gateway to your mountain top. It calls for honor and dignity. It will put your name in the Guinness Book of Records. According to Proverbs 18:16, it is a key to impossible doors of opportunities in life. It announces your name in the high places of the earth. It is your divine key to a divine connection. Talent drives you into the place of reputation and prestige. Life is not by your size, height, complexion or race. It is by what you can do to help humanity.

*"The spider taketh hold with her hands, and is in kings' palace"* (Proverbs 30:28)

When men say you are lazy, it may not truly be that you are lazy. You could be lazy in the sense that you are not able to do what they can do, but you have an ability they have not discovered. May God open your eyes in Jesus name!

Who were some of those that went to the mountain top of life, and what were their talents? Listen, you have a glorious future, but your natural talent(s) or spiritual gift(s) as a minister of God is your destiny car to your predestined future. So discover it.

## SOME OF THE PEOPLE THAT MADE IT TO THE MOUNTAIN TOP AND THEIR TALENTS

The phrase "mountain top" talks about the place of recognition.

1.  Joseph: his talent was administration. Even if he could interpret dreams but could not administer, he would have not gotten such a honorable and admirable position in his life.
2.  Jephthah: although he was rejected because he was taken for a nonentity, he became the president of his nation by virtue of his ability as a warrior (Judges 11-12:1-7).
3.  Hiram: he was a craftsman, who later became a man after Solomon's heart. How favorable it is to be a contractor chosen by a president of a nation as most preferred for handling of projects for the country of Israel.
4.  Gideon: a warrior who was a chief commandant or a chief of army staff.
5.  Solomon: he had an administrative ability. He was a wise king with an exceptional sense of judgment. He made a name above all kings who were in his time.

Talent changes your financial status. It puts money into your hands with time. A wise man said, "If you are poor, it is because you are trading nothing." Talent removes the shame of poor parental background. The discovery of **"Talent"** is the discovery of good future. It is the pivot around which your existence revolves. It is the myth behind all gains in life. Talent gives you a good name. The blindness of your mind towards your ability is the reason for your failure in life, and it will certainly put you in hiding. Your talent is your only road to a good future. It is the starting point of every good race to every good ending. It is the lens through which you see a good future. Whenever you think of how your talent will link you with a good financial and material possession, it will make you rejoice greatly. If you can grab your ability, you can celebrate your future. It calls for a conductive life.

Until you see your talent as a lion sees an antelope, you will not go forward. Your decision will be genuine if you have seen your 'antelope'. Your ignorance to your talent can call for a perpetual idleness, a major reason for poverty.

If people are neglecting you, separate yourself; discover your talent or ability, work upon it, and begin to release it. Those who neglected you will soon come back, bowing down to you (Isaiah 60:14, 15)

Talent is the beauty of destiny.

**Note:**

The four things to overlook when pursuing life are:

Tribe
Race
Stature
Age

So you must mind your talent or ability.

Man neglects carbon dioxide but plants need it for photosynthesis. Some people may be looked down upon with deep contempt, yet they may have great potentials within to help their generation, e.g. Jesus, who was termed the **"carpenter's son"** but became the Savior of the whole world.

As butter is for bread, so bread is for the body and body for the earth. Everything has its purpose for existing. God is not a fool. So know your importance and mind where you are needed.

Remember, there is no bad person on this earth that cannot be good. No matter how kola nut and bitter leaves are, those who need them are still discerning their importance. Even if the moon shines, the stars have their relevance. Do what you know best. A war that a warrior knows best cannot kill him. What you can do best will profit you better.

Remember, a king cannot be an orator when there are no people to listen to him. Use your talent in a place it will be welcomed, appreciated, celebrated and valued. Kola nut is small, but it will last long in the mouth of those who value it.

Why must you not fail in life? It is because you are loaded and seeded for success. You are God's replica. God is not a failure and he did not make you one.

I see you becoming successful in life as you discover your ability and talent in Jesus' name!

## B. FANNING INTO FLAME THE GIFT IN YOU

As I always say, every man is created to solve a problem for his generation. But many fail to wake up to embrace the fact that they are embodiments of solutions to certain problems of life. They have refused to believe that they are debtors to their generation.

Listen, you that is reading this book: the government, companies, private businesses and your society could be waiting for you, but if you refuse to wake up to the needs of your generation, you will definitely die unfulfilled. I therefore challenge you in the name of Jesus to rise from your slumber.

I see you welcomed in the sky of life as you arise. I see uproar of the shout of joy because of your rising like the morning sun, after years of your generation groping in the darkness of life or as dew falling upon the thirsty grasses of the field. I see the birds of the sky singing to the heavens as they see your rising. I see the crowd of weepers wiping off their long-running tears from their beautiful cheeks. I see the elements of the earth-moon, stars, sun, etc. blessing God from the bottom of their hearts because of you. Please rise up with your dreams and do something within the space of your short stay here on earth, that at the close of the day, heaven will count you worthy of rewards.

The gift of God inside you is not put in there for fancy. It is not for decoration.

*"Wherefore I put you in remembrance that thou stir up the gift of God, which is in thee . . . and stop being afraid, for God had not given us the spirit of fear . . . but of sound mind"* (2 Tim. 1:6,7, paraphrased)

Remember, life is not only based on spiritual gifts but also physical. Gifts and ministry are interwoven. They are inseparable. Ministry, according to my definition, is rendering of services. And it takes gifts to render services to people. God solves human problems through spiritual and physical means—gifts, talent and abilities of people. Your ministry could be political, economical, scientific, technological, business-wise or gospel-wise. You are just God's instrument through which He works his good deeds to the benefit of mankind. Remember, without God, nothing is possible.

## Why must we stir up the gift(s) in us?

1. It is your mandate from God. Make full proof of your ministry (2 Timothy 4:5)
2. Your generation needs it (1 Corinthians 12:8-30)
3. It is for the edification of Christ's body (Ephesians 4:12-14)
4. It is for profiting (Proverbs 14:23; I Corinthians 12:7)

## What are the profits?

1. Stirring your gifts up will make you grow great in them and with them (John 12:24)
2. It provokes material blessings (Proverbs 12:11, 14; 28:19; 18:20). So don't hide your gift

## How can you stir up your gift to make it profitable?

You only do this by being properly informed about it (Daniel 11:32; 12:3). To be informed is to have knowledge of a thing. Until you know properly how a thing functions, you will never make any headway with it.

## How can you be well informed?

Read books of people ahead of you in your area of endeavor. Prophet Daniel did this (Daniel 9:2). This will help you to magnify your office as Paul the Apostle did (1 Corinthians 7:20).

Read the book of the Law. It contains the wisdom keys with which to make success in life (Psalm 1:1-3; Joshua 1:8). We shall talk about this more in chapter seven.

**Note:** Study to know the technical know-how of your gift so you can avoid shame! Go to school; learn under the people ahead of you, both in knowledge and practical. I see God helping you!

In conclusion, whatever you never start will never grow (Job 8:7; Zechariah 4:9, 10). So start doing something about your gift and calling now.

# CHAPTER SIX

## SEPARATING ONTO A BETTER THING

*"THROUGH DESIRE, A MAN having separated himself seeketh and intermeddleth with all wisdom"* (Proverbs 18:1)

So many times in life, some people do ask themselves the following questions: **"Why am I facing this ridicule? Why is life hard for me, even when I am working? Why is my manager angry with me, even when I try to please him? Why is everybody in this company against me; and what have I done wrong?"** And sometimes, some are being sacked from their jobs without a cause.

To some, though they are working, nothing seems to be all right. This has brought about confusion, frustration and bitterness in the lives of many.

Some have hated themselves and, as a result, have committed suicide today. I bring good news to as many as are still in any of these categories. I see God lifting you out of that mess. May God's power set you free from that grip of suicide today! I see you conquering depression triumphantly by the blood of your covenant with God through Christ Jesus today!

As the word of God came to Joseph in his chains when he was in prison and delivered him, I see you coming out the same way from any unhappy situation the same way! Your announcement to your world has finally come today! Count it all joy for your encounter with this book in your life, for it is in divine program that you should come in touch with this truth to set you free from mental torture.

Until you locate or discover your destiny, you will never be organized in life. It takes the discovery of destiny to separate yourself from what you are not designed for.

Let us take a look at the men who fulfilled their destinies, and see how and what they separated from.

1. Moses: in Exodus chapter 1 and 2, he was born and was picked up by pharaoh's daughter, and was also brought up by them. But at a time, even when he was enjoying life, he had no peace, no rest of mind, and no joy and was not happy with what he was doing. This was because destiny was calling for him. At a time in his life, he was deceived and was crowned with the crown of fake destiny, which was not in the direction of his divine destiny, and would have never been able to see his true glory, if not for the help of God.

He was made a prince, a position that many would have termed opportunity, but he later discovered that he was not made to be where he was.

Now see his account: *"By faith Moses, when he was come to age, refused to be called the son of Pharaoh's daughter; knowing who he was. He chose rather to suffer affliction with the people of God (knowing his destiny as a leader, who was born to bring them out of Egypt), than to enjoy the pleasures of sin for a season. By faith he forsook Egypt, not fearing the wrath of the king: for he endured, as seeing him who is invisible [who revealed to him his destiny]"* (Hebrews 11:24, 25, 27, paraphrased).

That is the same way God will separate you this year to encounter the best for your life in Jesus' name!

2. Jeremiah: to him God said, *"Before I formed thee in the belly I knew thee; and before thou comest forth out of the womb I sanctified thee, and I ordained thee a prophet unto the nations"* (Jeremiah 1:5)

71

To be sanctified is to be set apart. And to be ordained is to be commissioned.

To my understanding, this young man, Jeremiah, could be thinking about what he would do as a youth without consulting his maker. But God in his infinite mercy appeared to him and said to him, "My Son, I wondered what you must be thinking about yourself. Why must you reduce yourself to be what you are not born for? Your make-up is not of a carpenter or a lawyer. Although you are very intelligent, you are not carrying the grace and ability of a manager nor of an architect. So before you destroy your life by malfunctioning, let me tell you who you are. You are designed, favored and empowered to only be a prophet to the nations."

This is being separated divinely onto a better thing. Every man needs this kind of encounter with the God of heaven by revelation. The only prayer you need to pray should be: "Lord, reveal myself to me. Separate me from what my fulfillment is not attached to, and connect me to my purpose and destiny." I see God answering this prayer for you this year!

3.  Peter: in Mark chapter one verse sixteen and seventeen, Jesus met Peter as a fisherman. Although he was very good in it, it still did not prevent Jesus from telling him his destiny: **"Follow me, and I will make you fisher of men."**

That you learnt a skill does not mean it is your destiny. Get your approval and assurance from God, who made you. Can't you see that when Peter became a preacher, his life made a history and has affected, and is still affecting, the whole world? Check his records in the bible and see his full account (Acts 3, 4, 5, 8-12).

4.  Paul: this is another man I so cherish. He was a Jewish philosopher and the son of a philosopher, and studied under the greatest philosopher of his time—Gamaliel. But in the midst of his duty, carrying out the instruction of the government of his time and as a very zealous and faithful servant, Jesus appeared to him and caused him the change of direction, which led to the fulfillment of his life and purpose. Praise God!

Look at what he said, *"For ye have heard of my conversation in time past in the Jews' religion, how that beyond measure I persecuted the Church of God, and wasted it: and profited in the Jews' religion above many my equals in my own nation, being more exceedingly zealous of the traditions of my fathers"* (Galatians 1:13, 14).

But when the time for divine separation came, Jesus appeared to him on his way to Damascus, where he was going to fulfill the king's command, and spoke to him in the Hebrews tongue. That you don't understand English language is never an excuse. God will speak to you in the language you will understand!

Let us hear Paul's testimony about his separation: *"At midday, O king, I saw in the way a light from heaven, above the brightness of the sun, shining round about me and them which journeyed with me. And when we were all fallen to the earth, I heard a voice speaking unto me, and saying in the Hebrews tongue, Saul, Saul, why persecutest thou me? It is hard for thee to kick against the pricks. And I said, Who art thou, Lord? And he said, I am Jesus whom thou persecutest. But rise, and stand upon thy feet: for I have appeared unto thee for this purpose, to make thee a minister and a witness both to these things which thou hast seen and of those things in the which I will appear unto thee; delivering thee from the people, and from the Gentiles unto whom now I send thee, to open their eyes, and to turn them from darkness to light, and from the power of Satan unto God, that they may receive forgiveness of sins, and inheritance among them which are sanctified by faith that is in me"* (Acts 26:13-19). What an encounter!

And finally, Paul showed his bold step and determination by saying, *"Whereupon, O king Agrippa, I was not disobedient unto the heavenly vision"* (Acts 26:19).

It is good to encounter God, but be willing to give heed to the power of his wind of separation—instruction.

5.  Philip: this young man was ordained as a deacon in the Church, but that was a capital ridicule and limitation on his divine destiny. I give praise to God, who separated him onto his real honorable and foreordained office as an Evangelist, and gave him four

daughters who became prophetesses after the commencement of the persecution on the Church at Jerusalem. Read Acts 8; 21:8, 9.

Joseph: the story of Joseph is another awesome and encouraging story of destiny. You can't preach on destiny without mentioning his name. In his case, it was a change of location from a pit to slavery, then to prison, where he made use of his gift that made his way to the top of life. Thank God for his brothers who persecuted him to the place of fulfillment! You need this kind of separation.

Maybe why your boss is persecuting you is because God wants to move you to a better place and to a better thing. Who knows?

Time will not permit me to mention a man like Abraham, who was born in a land where he was never to be fulfilled. And God took him to a place where he had riches and over 300 (three hundred) servants.

This year, God must separate you from your worries and put you in the place where you will meet with the right job for your destiny in order to be fulfilled.

Remember, there are so many talents today that do not have their course study in the present day institutions, depending on the country you are living in. Discover your own and work on it. Jesus is on your side!

**Things that will make you not to locate your destiny**

1. Sin (Isaiah 59:1, 2)
2. Wrong environment
3. Societal influences—which can make you to be inspired to do the only thing you are seeing people doing except by God's love and intervention.
4. Parental influences: this is where your parent imposes on you a thing that is not meant for you without your ability to refuse it.
5. Relatives' pressure or influences
6. Inheritance mentality
7. Inability to follow God's direction
8. Doubting God's revelation or vision shown to you
9. Fear of want and lack
10. Lack of confidence in God

11. Fear of oppositions, etc.

## AVOIDING THE DISTRACTIONS OF LIFE

No distracted person succeeds in life; rather he or she will always be confused. Some major accidents are caused by a confused mind. Some divorces are caused by the confusion of the mind.

A confused person is a troublesome person. Confusion of the mind can cause unnecessary major quarrels. A confused mind is an unfocused mind. All kinds of ideas flow into it, whether good or bad. It lays blame on others as the source of its predicament. Anger and bitterness are products of a confused mind.

Jesus said, *"The light of the body is the eye: therefore when thine eye is single, the whole body also is full of light; but when thine eye is evil, thy body is full of darkness. Take heed therefore that the light which is in thee be not darkness"* (Luke 11:34, 35).

Jesus here is talking about concentration and double-mindedness. "Mind" is a gift on its own. Wisdom functions speedily in a settled mind. When you know where you are going, and what it takes to get there, and put your hands on deck diligently, your success is sure.

If you don't want to be confused in life, you have to be aware of the following:

1. Understand what God wants you to do in this life.

2. Understand how he wants you to do it.

When you don't know these things, you will be struggling for another thing or doing what God wants you to do in a way outside of his will for you. This will keep you stagnated and frustrated when things are not moving for you. Ralph Mahoney, the founder of World Map, said, **"God's work, done in God's way, and in God's time, will never lack God's provision."**

Furthermore, confident talk and settlement in life are products of locating what God has attached your life and your peace to. So you must find it out, for *"It is the glory of God to conceal a thing: but the honour of kings to search out a matter"* (Proverbs 25:2). May God help you in Jesus name!

3. Find out where God wants you to do it.

4. Close your ears from people's suggestions that do not go in line with what God told you. Even if respected men of God advise you, seek God's face and follow the leading in your spirit based on your conviction. Until you are fully convinced to do a thing and you are sure it is God's will for you, don't do it.

5. Avoid the pressure of people's intimidations like, "They will not take you in that job; you are not qualified for it." Whatever God tells you to do, do it. Never listen to people that always want to define you by your inabilities but listen to God, who can only define you by your abilities. Trust in God. He will never deceive you.

I have suffered in God's hand and have cried tearlessly because of listening to wrong suggestions. When you allow confusion to govern your mind, your life will come to a standstill at the junction of life. May God keep you from being confused!

Worry is one of the defects that affect a confused mind, and worry results to mental fatigue. This is a blockage to mental excellence. When you allow worry to pervade your mind, positive reasoning will be impossible. This is why people get stuck in life.

Talking about the major distractions of life, anything that has power to command your attention from your God-given vision has power to dominate your finance and time, and can also control your destiny and thwart your divine plan.

The two major things that I have discovered too distracting in life are as follows:

1. Unnecessary pleasure

*"Drinking makes you forget your responsibilities, and you mistreat the poor. Beer and wine are only for the dying or for those who have lost hope.*

*Let them drink and forget how poor and miserable they feel"* (Proverbs 31:5-7)

These are the words that king Lemuel's mother told him. Kings are simply great men. You can't aspire to be great and still ply the road where the mean are found. The airplane that tends to fly successfully needs not to press the north button and still take the route going to the south. Drinking makes your vision to derail.

*"But they also have erred through wine, and through strong drink are out of the was . . . they err in vision . . ."* (Isaiah 28:7).

Vision simply means having an insight into the realities of life, either concerning you or concerning others.

Many think that vision is only reserved for the priests and prophets. This is not true. By virtue of redemption, once you are born again, you are entitled to receive revelation(s) from God—this is called vision.

According to 1Corinthians 2:9-10, the Holy Spirit reveals to us God's mind. But know this, the Holy Spirit and strong drinks are like two parallel lines. Please run away from strong drinks.

2.   Living in immorality.

Words like mind, life, and soul are alike. The purity of the mind is like the pinhole of a camera that has no dirt. The manufacturer of man, who knows what can spoil his product, said that man should avoid sexual immorality. It is only a sound mind that can receive vision from God. And a sound mind is a product of the Spirit of God (2 Timothy 1:7).

Remember, man is the temple of the Holy Ghost, who is the giver of visions to a sound mind. So, automatically, when sexual immorality is committed, the Holy Ghost departs from a man, thereby causing him to lose the soundness of his mind—the place of divine vision.

No mind is sound until it is enveloped by the power of the Holy Spirit. So when this power leaves, the mind becomes dead to the things of God. Then tell me how you can still retain your God-given vision when the life of the vision (God's Spirit) is departed.

Look at these Scriptures: *"To deliver thee from the strange woman, even from the stranger that flattereth with her words, which forsaketh the guide of her youth, and forgetteth the covenant of her God. For her house inclineth unto death, and her paths unto the dead. None that go unto her return again, neither take they hold of the paths of life"* (Proverbs 2:16-19).

*"Whoso loveth wisdom rejoiceth his father: but he that keepeth company with harlorts spendeth his substance"* (Proverbs 29:3)

*"If you love wisdom your parents will be glad, but chasing after bad women will cost you everything"* (Proverbs 29:3, C.I.V)

When you pursue after women, your attention will be divided. And when you make love to a woman, your soul **"life or blood"** cleaves to her (Genesis 34:1-3). Remember; Jesus said, **"Where your treasure is, there will your heart be also."** So you can't pursue after women without your substance going with it. Be careful! This has ruined the destinies of many great people. May the power of God keep you in Jesus' name!

There was a man who was born to be great and live an excellent life, but when his father, Jacob, at his old age, called all his sons in order to tell them what would befall them, he said to him, *"Reuben, thou art my firstborn, my might, and the beginning of my strength, the excellency of dignity, and the excellency of power. Unstable as water, thou shalt not excel; because thou wentest up to thy father's bed; then defiledst thou it: he went up to my couch"* (Genesis 49:3, 4).

This means that you will never see greatness because you are morally loose. You easily fall to the tune of woman sexually.

I believe that this is not the way you are. If it is, better seek the intervention of God in your life. And I believe God will see you through in Jesus' mighty name!

If you are under such captivity, by the unction of God on me, I command the spirit of immorality to come out of you now in Jesus' name!

## Keys for overcoming sexual immorality

No person suddenly falls into sexual immorality unprepared mentally and emotionally. Before this evil comes your way, there are steps you must obey if really you want to overcome it. This is because the battle starts from casual indulgences. So in order to avoid this evil act, obey the following rules; they are under **"The principle of the mind and actions"**.

1. Don't lust after the physical make-up (facial beauty). of the opposite sex
2. Don't imagine the physical physique of the opposite sex in your mind. Remember, what you think is what you feel, and if it enters your emotion, it will certainly conquer your will power unless you know the subsequent repercussions and are able to cast down the imagination and pull down its strongholds in your mind and emotion and bring to subject such thought to the obedience of Christ.
3. Avoid casual visitations. That is, going alone to the house of an opposite sex. If you do, you will be surprised with what you may experience—either the person's lustful actions toward you or your lustful actions toward the person. The end may be shameful.
4. Avoid any casual relationship that may certainly lead you into sexual immorality.
5. Remember, males are easily controlled by what they see, while females are easily controlled by the sweet words and the romantic touches of men. So control yourself before these things control you. Avoid the practice of the admiration of females' look, as a male. Don't listen to the luring words of males nor allow their touches on your body, as a female, observing their immoral intentions towards you.
6. Don't be too close to immoral people, either in Church or outside the Church. Unknown to you, they can be after you.
7. Avoid being sentimental about immoral issues (things like he or she is just a friend), because the devil is watching out for an opportunity against your destiny.
8. When anybody is making suspicious advances towards you, avoid them, and pretend not to have noticed them.

9.  Be very careful of accepting financial or material gifts from the opposite sex. This is why you must be hard-working in order to fend for yourself.

10. Especially as a male, don't allow females embracing you unnecessarily. That is a medium to play harlotry on you. Be careful! Don't allow anyone to tell you immoral stories. What you hear affects your thought and your night dreams. Your thought affects your feelings and decisions. I have always said this.

11. Never feed and arouse your sexual emotion by watching sexual movies, reading books or periodicals that contain sexual stories and pornographic pictures. These can put you under the control of your emotions. Even as a married person, it may lead you to adultery, most especially when your spouse is not around (Proverbs 4:23; Philippians 4:8). Stop placing pornographic calendars on your room walls. Guide your eyes from those things. They will stir up your sexual emotion and eventually lead you into sin. You cannot control your emotions without God's help. So, control the members of your body—eyes, ears, hands and legs. Remember, anytime your thought has been geared toward sexuality and its temperature level reaches its highest peak, you will have no option than to release the vapor.

12. When you notice any thought of lust about the opposite sex or naked picture of the opposite sex coming into your mind, don't think on it. Rebuke it and the power behind it; and cast it off your mind immediately with prayers. They are demonic projections. Don't neglect them. If they find a way into your subconscious, you will be in trouble. Never fail to speak in spiritual tongues when you notice such things coming into your mind. This helps to dispel any demonic imaginations from your mind too.

13. Avoid sleeping passing the night the house of an opposite sex— somebody that is not your husband or wife.

14. When the devil brings an immoral dream to you, as soon as you wake up, pray against it, even in tongues in the Holy Ghost, for at least five minutes.

15. Always read the Bible in the morning when you wake up, and in the evening before going to bed. This will help you a great deal to control your mind and feelings (John 15:3; Ephesians 5:26).

16. Learn to make a positive relationship that is beneficial to you and your destiny, if you really want to be fulfilled.
17. Live a life of prayer always. One word you may hear from God when praying will keep your mind sanctified always.
18. When the Holy Ghost reveals the immoral thoughts in the mind of someone towards you, don't try to find out if it is true by trying the person. If you do, you will open the door for the person immediately, and if such person is the very fast type, he or she will get at you before you know it. Just believe the Holy Ghost and stay far from the person, and be very watchful in prayer, following these rules given to you. God bless you!

**Note:** As a single male, don't allow a female to take care of your domestic activities except if she is your fiancée, if you can behave wisely before her.

## THE PILLARS OF FAILURE

How do I know who will never succeed in the pursuit of his or her God-given vision?

There are some practical steps in life I have found destructive when pursuing success; and I will just simply state them here:

1. Lack of critical survey of the possibility of a vision (1 Thessalonians 5:21). Find out the "where", "how" and "when" it can work.
2. Moral indiscipline
3. Covetousness (Proverbs 28:16; 1Timothy 6:9, 10; Proverbs 28:20, 22)
4. Slothfulness towards the necessity to achieve purpose
5. Time mismanagement
6. Lack of concentration (Songs of Solomon 1:6)
7. Employing a non-teachable spirit
8. Wrong relationships (Proverbs 13:20).
9. Slothfulness (Proverbs. 12:27). That is, not putting ideas to work.
10. Lazy attitude
11. Indecisiveness

12. Lack of planning (Proverbs 24:27). A wise man said, **"If you fail to plan, you have planned to fail."**
13. Lack of faith in oneself and in God
14. Fear of stepping out (Proverbs 22:13)
15. Financial indiscipline
16. Lack of mentorship (Proverbs 15:22)
17. Lack of proper and right information about one's pursuit
18. Fear of delegation
19. Fear of competition from followers
20. Procrastination
21. Fear of mistakes or failure in pursuit of one's dream

Excuses

Anyone pressing any of those buttons will never see the top of the mountain. May wisdom lead you in life in Jesus' name (Ecclesiastes 10:10)!

# THE INSTRUMENTS FOR DESTINY ENHANCEMENT

There are two things that intensively affect a man's destiny. They may either improve it or fray it.

RELATIONSHIP: *"He that walketh with wise men shall be wise: but a companion of fools shall be destroyed" (Proverbs13:20).* Your relationships in life will simply determine your focus, the height you can attain in life, the information you acquire, your meditation, your level of understanding and your attitude.

*"Be not deceived: evil communications corrupt good manners"* (1 Corinthians 15:33)

There is no relationship without communication. Every communication has an effect on the mind of a man. And remember, whatever enters your heart through your ears and goes through the process of autosuggestion has power to manifest out of you. This is why a man is subject to changes in life. Your dream in life can only survive under the atmosphere of good and positive relationships.

Dreams are easily frayed by the deceptive advice of vain friends. The bible says, *"He that tilleth his land shall have plenty of bread: but he that followeth after vain persons shall have poverty enough"* (Proverbs 28:19).

You can't relate with time wasters and still remain on the road to success in life. But there are some people in life that you come in contact with, your life and vision will encounter a positive turn-around and speed. God will connect you with such people in your life in Jesus' precious name!

## Why do you need relationship in your life?

You need relationship because you must climb on someone's shoulder to see farther. Mentorship is a major bridge to tomorrow's success; it is the difference between a failure and a success. It is the line between a mediocre and a mentally improved person, because mentors are banks of information, while good colleagues are wonderful sharpeners (Proverbs 27:17).

Again, you need relationship because the word of God says that two are better than one (Ecclesiastes 4:9, 10, 12; Dan. 2:16, 17, 19-20, 22).

## Factors that destroy beneficial relationship

1. Pride: its fuel is ignorance. How do you know a proud person? a. He looks down on others. b. He does not regard the work of others. c. He does not respect people who are lower than he financially. d. He counts on age so much that anywhere he goes; he wants to know how old you are. He hardly greets. e. He hates to be controlled by others who are higher than him because he hardly believes anyone is higher than him. f. He likes to talk down on people or runs others down with his mouth in order to elevate himself. g. He never obeys the principles of others. He is full of his own ways or of himself.

## The results of pride

1. It leads to great fall (Proverbs 16:18)
2. It leads to wickedness (having a wicked heart)
3. It births resistance from God (James 4:6)

4.  God brings you down
5.  It does not bring you promotion
6.  It creates enemies around you
7.  You may lose your place in life, your job or your position
8.  Insincerity / dishonesty
9.  Lack of concern for others
10. Having no value for others. That is, not counting on other's personality
11. Ingratitude
12. Intimidating attitude/character assassination
13. Untrustworthiness
14. Unfaithfulness
15. It separates you from worthy and competent friends

Let's continue on the factors that can destroy beneficial relationship:

2.  Carelessness based on lack of respect or insensitivity to people's principles. For example: carelessness in relating with mentors, lack of respect for people's personal programs, not careful in managing people's properties, carelessness in choosing words, not careful in dealing with customers or clients, etc.

3.  Sentimentalism: being casual in your attitude toward people and despising the little things that matter all in the name of "we are very close" or "I know him or her very well; so there will be no problem." This leads to using casual languages that provoke without the user noticing; taking away someone's properties without seeking the person's permission. Sentiment can make you take people for granted.

4.  Indiscipline: a disciplined person can never follow nor agree with undisciplined persons (Amos 3:3). Indiscipline can easily cause problems between two individuals.

A disciplined person is a person that has self-control with good and profitable principles. An undisciplined person hates correction, he hates to see friends that have rules and regulations; he doesn't obey protocol. He is easily angry when corrected. He sees those who have principles as proud. He is very foolish, arrogant and proud. He can easily enter into trouble because of insensitivity to order, and carelessness in his manners and verbal expressions. He talks before he reasons instead of the other way round. He is easily controlled by negative emotions—anger, lust, over happiness, appetite and the first sight of things and people. He spends unwisely.

5.  Lack of integrity: never truthful or trustworthy. This kind of a person is also known to be fraudulent, tricky, unfaithful to his words, or telling cock-and-bull stories to gain the interest or approval of others. The later can be very fatal, because when you are caught, you will definitely lose your honor and the respect.

Anytime you fail your promises or breach a contract (between you and people), never hesitate to apologize to the party/parties involved. You should try as much as possible to gain their forgiveness by being frank. Never fail promises unless there is obstruction by an impromptu occurrence(s) above your control.

**Note:** The people that lack integrity usually lack moral uprightness. They are so defensive and full of excuses that are not cogent enough. They are never apologetic. They never accept their error(s), even when proven to have committed the offences alleged against them. They are always wise in their own conceit. They are full of their own ways.

6.  Lack of moral uprightness: this kind of person lacks good manner of speech, does not respect elders, despises people, is very proud and arrogant and is lawless. He has a very bad habit of eating, lacks the good manner of approach, is very selfish, always indifferent to people's feelings, is unsympathetic and uncompassionate, is unapproachable, non-teachable and uncontrollable or ungovernable, lacks home training, mal-handles his subordinates, and is full of wicked devices. These kinds of people are very deceptive like a chameleon.

## How to maintain a good relationship

1.  Avoid friends that are questionable
2.  Avoid talebearers (Proverbs 11:13; 26:20; 16:28)
3.  Avoid foolish persons (Proverbs 14:7).
4.  Don't reveal secrets (Proverbs 25:9, 10; 11:13)

5. Bear one another's burden (Gal. 6:12, 10; Proverbs 17:17)
6. Do good to each other (Ephesians 6:7, 8; Proverbs 3:37)
7. Be a problem solver to each other (Proverbs 18:24)
8. Be a source of inspiration (build one another up mentally in a positive way)

**Note:** You should be sensitive enough to understand who is above you enough to be your mentor; who you should relate with as a colleague; and who you should you should relate with as your protégé.

### Other purposes for relationships

1. for restoration
2. for motivation
3. for strength
4. for inspiration

### Character: the tool that makes success possible

Everybody is born to succeed. You may have all it takes to succeed—money, good ideas, helpers, etc., but if you have a character flaw, you will never go far in life.

The possible link road to success is a good relationship between you and God, and between you and people that matter to your destiny.

Monkeys display their jumping expertise successfully and enjoyably because trees with connective branches are close to each other; without which you cannot discover the abilities of a monkey. This is a practical example of the power of network. If you can understand the cobwebs of a spider, you will understand the power of a good network. Businesses in today's world are progressing geometrically because of advanced human and technological network.

A good relationship is one of the true keys to success in life and endeavor. No man is an island. Even God Himself is not alone. There are three personalities in one God. And these personalities work together to make things possible.

There must be good relationship between friends, husbands and wives, business partners, a businessman and his customers and workers, a person and his or her family, etc. The key to this good relationship is a good character.

So many people are sacked from their jobs and others are disappointed in their prospective jobs because of character flaws. The reason why many people are character deficient is because of the lack of a good child upbringing.

ENVIRONMENT: as in relationship, environment is another factor that will determine the enhancement of your destiny. Whether you believe it or not, there is a place you will be, you will never experience the beauty of life.

You need God to position you in the place of your blossoming. If you are not there yet, I pray that God will take you there in Jesus' name!

This factor calls for a divine direction (Deuteronomy 32:10-13). Read Genesis 26:1-5, 11-14. See how God's directive instruction made a wealthy man out of Isaac in the days of depression (economic recession). The Lord will help you too! Your destiny will not be wasted!

To every divine assignment, there is a divine geographical location (Genesis 12: 1-3). Remember the story of Joseph and his dreams! His dreams only came through as he entered the land of Egypt. Remember Daniel in Babylon! Remember Esther in a foreign land! Remember Philip in Samaria! There is always a place where your destiny will be fulfilled. Don't forget that apple does not grow everywhere!

## THE POSITIVE KEYS FOR FOCUS

Focus is one of the master keys to success. It is known as having total control of the mind and directing it to the area of positive intelligence.

Many people have visions of their future but not many people pursue their visions successfully. Among the numerous reasons why they couldn't succeed is lack of focus. Solomon understood this. As a man of experience in the midst of many distractions that came his way, he gave us a wonderful counsel:

*"Keep thy heart with all diligence; for out of it are the issues of life. Let thine eyes look right on, and let thine eyelids look straight before thee. Ponder the path of thy feet, and let all thy ways be established. Turn not to the right hand, nor to the left: remove thy foot from evil"* (Proverbs 4:23, 25-27)

Every divine success begins with a divine vision of a divine plan or purpose of God for a man. But this takes place in the mind.

As I said before now, vision simply means insight into a divine plan. A typical example of having a vision is recorded in Jeremiah chapter one. In verse five, God showed Jeremiah who he was and what service he was to render to his generation. In verse thirteen, God showed him the nature of his prophetic ministry, which was a judgment make-up. He was to constantly tell Jerusalem what would always befall them as they kept going astray from God. The question that God asked him was, **'What seest thou?'** This was not a physical sight but spiritual, through the eyes of his mind. This question now comes to you, **'What seest thou?' 'What are you seeing in your future?'** Are you seeing anything at all? If you are not seeing, you are emphatically living a meaningless life. But if you are seeing anything at all, I want to let you know that it doesn't end in seeing, but it must be governed by the power of focus.

Keep this at the back of your mind: the devil is a vision or dream killer. He does so by blinding your mental eyes with negative influences. If he succeeds in blinding your mind from your vision, he can master your destiny.

## HOW TO OVERCOME WORRY, SORROW AND ANXIETY

The mind is the most powerful asset to humanity. Every sense that anything can make in this life is because it came as a product of a sound, dynamic and creative mind.

As I said earlier, everything we do in life begins from our mind. If there is anything so far in life that I immensely and jealously show appreciation towards God for, I think it should be that he only did not make man but also, without hesitation, gave man the most needed and valued factor called **'The mind'**. The mind is the source of and basement for every human activity.

**The major functions of the mind**

**Inspiration:** if you have grasped the idea of what God wants you to do in your life, it happened by the inspiration of God in the womb of your spirit called **'Mind'**.

*"But there is a spirit in man: and the inspiration of the Almighty giveth them understanding"* (Job 32:8)

**Meditation:** this is the power of the mind that can be invoked into place, when a man gets an idea or a vision from God. It is to engage the satellite of the mind to get a better insight or call it understanding in what the vision really entails through divine illumination.

*"Meditate upon these things (vision), give thyself wholly to them; that thy profiting may appear to all"* (1 Timothy 4:15, Paraphrased)

What you don't understand, you don't pursue; what you can't or do not pursue, you can't prove to your generation. It is your duty to make your calling or election sure (2Peter 1:10, 11); and without this, you will never make profit out of it.

Look at this Scripture carefully:

*"We have also a more sure word of prophecy (the word of God that came unto you); whereunto ye do well that ye take heed, as unto a light that shineth in a dark place, until the day dawn, and the day star arise in your hearts"* (2 Peter 1:19 Paraphrased)

This scripture absolutely reveals to us that God's word that may come to us can only come as just a beam of light. It will take our duty to engage the power of meditation, brooding over the arrived word that comes into our dark hearts, so it can bring us to the exactly understanding of what God is saying to us. This will make us jump up on our feet to carry out or run with the vision as the star of our destiny begins to shine in our mind; that is, having a clear picture of what life will be to us in the future as we run with God's vision.

**Imagination:** this can also be called "image formation". It is the ability to see in pictures what God is showing you by his Spirit. This kind of vision cannot be easily forgotten. This is the most powerful factor of the mind that causes you or enables you to bring your future closer to yourself. It helps you to clearly define your vision to others who are like-minded.

**Understanding:** when a man's thinking faculty or sixth sense has been fully employed to reason over information or a matter, which can best take place in a quiet environment or atmosphere, the truth of the whole matter opens up like an eruption of volcanoes and makes the information factual, and also causes joy to rise up on his inside. This end-point is called 'Understanding', which brings about an assurance of the workability of an idea as the visionary begins to see the future result of such idea; especially an idea that comes from heaven as a purpose delivered to him or her to live with. It is like a full light that sheds over the mind of someone, leaving no trace of doubt in him.

**Thinking:** this is the line between a success and a failure. We have positive and negative thinking. Thinking is trying to analyze or curiously dig deep mentally on the **'why'**, **'how'** and **'when'** of a matter. It is also called reasoning or planning mentally within you or with a group of people graphically on what, how and when an idea should be carried out and thereby programming such a plan (that is, tagging time to priorities). This function helps you to carefully and wisely identify the location suitable to implement a discovered idea as the Lord helps you. It will work for you too!

Having successfully discovered the major functions of the most wonderful human asset—the mind—that God has given to us, which is applicable for the success and prosperity of our divine pursuit in life, I will like to unfold to you the likely identified demonic viruses that can destroy these virtues of the mind and also blind it from keeping sight of the future:

1. Depression—the down-casting of the mind that reduces it excellence.

2.  Sorrow—a deep regret or distress cause by loss or disappointment. It has the capacity to ruin one's psyche and render one's mental prowess inactive.
3.  Worry—this is self tormenting. It is to suffer oneself with disturbing thoughts. It leads to anxiety.
4.  Anxiety—having uncertainty of the future. It is also called psychiatry—a state of apprehension occurring in some forms of mental disorder. It is mentally destructive.
5.  Bitterness—intense anger over someone or a matter. It leads to resentment, and it is characterized by intense antagonism or hostility.

## How do they come?

These are negative factors that can be easily invited to war against the positive and beneficial factors of the mind unknowingly, which the devil organizes against humanity in order to mute the plans of God for their lives. And these negative factors come through the following:

1.  Anger over setbacks
2.  Constant expression of unhappiness over past failure, not willing to forgive oneself; holding unto the past pains.
3.  Anxiety is caused by lack of vision of one's purpose for living.
4.  Disappointments from people that was once trusted (Proverbs 13:12)
5.  Poverty (A poor man is an angry man).
6.  Greed for gains (1 Tim. 6:9, 10).
7.  Comparison
8.  Taking criticisms personal
9.  Seeking people's approval and not God's approval (Gal. 1:16; Luke 6:26)
10. Fault finding attitude
11. An unforgiving attitude

These are major negative factors or influences that militate against mental excellence.

**Note:** major bitterness is a product of envy, unforgiving heart, and disappointments from trusted individuals as you experience breach of contract, failure in any form, mockery and criticism against one's success. These destabilize the mind and divert it from being focused on one's purpose in life. They are capable of draining off your joy—the live wire of vision and also the booster of positive mental attitude. Nothing boosts the reception of inspirations like joy.

## Scriptural connection between the mind, mouth and life

These Scriptures are pointers to warnings, making us be conscious of demonic manipulations that tend to make us destroy our destinies with our own mouths through negative thinking:

*". . . For out of the abundance of the heart the mouth speaketh . . . For by thy words thou shalt be justified, and by thy words thou shalt be condemned"* (Matthew 12:34b, 37)

*". . . Looking diligently lest any man fall of the grace of God; lest any root of bitterness springing up trouble you . . ."* (Hebrews 12:15)

*"A merry heart doeth good like a medicine: but a broken spirit drieth the bones"* (Proverbs 17:22)

*"The heart knoweth its own bitterness; and a stranger doth not intermeddle with his joy"* (Proverbs 14:10)

*"Even in laughter the heart is sorrowful; and the end of that mirth is heaviness"* (Proverbs 14:13)

*"A sound heart is the life of the flesh: but envy the rottenness of the bones"* (Proverbs 14:30)

*"The spirit of a man will sustain his infirmity; but a wounded spirit who can bear"* (Proverbs 18:14)

*"Heaviness in the heart of a man maketh it stoop: but a good word maketh it glad"* (Proverbs 12:25)

*"A merry heart maketh a cheerful countenance: but by sorrow of the heart the spirit is broken"* (Proverbs 15:13)

*"A wholesome tongue is a tree of life: but perverseness therein is a breach in the spirit"* (Proverbs 15:4)

Explaining the scriptures respectively, it reads that destiny can be condemned by wrong use of one's mouth. Don't allow depression, bitterness, anxiety and sorrow to make you talk negatively. This can make God destroy the work of your hands (Ecclesiastes 5:6; Proverbs 6:2). Remember, God is in the business of doing what you say (Numbers 14:28)!

Be careful, a perverse tongue deprives the mind of having insight clearly. It causes a breach in the spirit. And again, if you allow your heart (spirit) to break, you are bound to be sick and be mentally depressed always. Be careful of what you allow into your mind!

## Effects of the absence of joy in a man's life

Joy is the major catalyst in the school of success. If it dies, life dies. Apostle Paul commanded us by the Holy Spirit to rejoice always. Even in the midst of all odds, this man, Paul, was joyful. And he said, *"In all things, give thanks unto God (1 Thessalonians 5:18)."* He also commanded us to rejoice in hope (Romans 12:12).

James, one of the Apostles, also commanded us likewise to count it all joy when we fall into diverse temptations (troubles of all sort). That is, the trial of our faith that works patience, which is the key to acquiring God's promises for us (James 1:24; Hebrews 10:35-35).

This is the secret of these great men of success. So I think there is need to follow their steps.

Let's look at the effects of the lack of joy in one's life from the following scripture:

*"Because thou servedst not the Lord thy God with joyfulness, and with gladness of heart, for the abundance of all things; therefore shalt thou serve thine enemies which the Lord shalt send against thee, in hunger, and in thirst, and in nakedness, and in want of all things: and he shall put a yoke of iron upon thy neck, until he have destroyed thee"* (Deuteronomy 28:47, 48)

If God puts a yoke on you, whose anointing will break it?

Everything can dry up in your life and destiny (favor, inspirations, progress—the product of inspiration, etc.).

*"The vine is dried up, and the fig tree languisheth; the pomegranate tree, the palm tree also, and the apple tree, even all the trees of the field, are withered: because joy is withered away from the sons of men"* (Joel 1:12)

May your joy never wither!

This kind of joy is not natural but divine. It is the gift of God as one of the fruits of the Holy Spirit. It is never easy to rejoice in the midst of problem like Paul and Silas' kind of trouble in the prison. It is the work of the Holy Spirit.

I pray God to give you this kind of joy now in Jesus' name!

This joy unravels to you the deep things of God by the Holy Spirit concerning your purpose and destiny.

You need to see through! Remember, until you see through, you can't breakthrough. It is what you see beyond the mountain that propels you to be willing to go through the mountain.

**Cure**

Let's look at the remedies for a biased mind:

1. Give thanks to God always, both for the good and for the bad (Job 23:10; 14:14; Habakkuk 3:17-19; Psalm 67:5, 6; 1 Thessalonians 5:18). Refuse to neither complain nor murmur (1 Corinthians 10:10).
2. Have an unshakable faith in what God has told you so far (Romans 4:17-21; Hebrews 11:7; Colossians 1:23).
   Stop discussing your pains. Forget your past (Isaiah 43:18, 19).
3. Avoid comparison. Understand that the glory of the sun, moon and the stars are not equal and does not have the same destiny or functions towards humanity (2 Corinthians 10:12-15).
4. Don't listen to critics. Understand that they are confused people, who never made it. So, seeing your success, they are provoked. They will only criticize you because they are afraid of you and do not understand the secrets behind your success.

5.  Avoid finding faults, knowing that no man is perfect (Matthew 7:1-5; 2 Timothy 2:25-26).

6.  Obtain a vision of your future and your divine purpose in life (Romans 8:28-29; Proverbs 29:18; 4:18; 15:30 Ecclesiastes 6:9).

7.  Look out for God's promises regarding your situation (Isaiah 34:16).

8.  Understand that your situation may be that you are crossing the bridges, deserts or wilderness along the road leading to the destination of your desired haven. No cross: no crown; no pressure: no pleasure; no fire: no gold (Proverbs 27:21).

9.  Depend on God's grace for your life. Remember that you have a colorful destiny, but it cannot be gotten by power or by might (1 Samuel 2:9; Zach.4: 6).

10. Remove your trust from man to avoid men's disappointment.

11. Believe God to bring your dream (his revelation of your tomorrow) to pass (Ezekiel 12:22-25).

12. Be filled with God's spirit (Isaiah 61:3, 4)

13. Be compulsorily joyful (Habakkuk 3:17-19; Nehemiah 8:10; James 5:13). Until you are merry, you cannot give thanks to God, through praise and worship, in your life (Zach. 14:17-18).

14. Stop asking yourself questions you cannot answer. Remember, life is a mystery. Only God can explain it.

# CHAPTER SEVEN

## TRAINING: THE INDISPENSABLE PLACE IN DESTINY

To START WITH, WHAT is training? It is the present continuous term for the word "train".

The dictionary meaning for **"training"** is the process of teaching or learning a skill, etc.

Also, the phrase "to train" means "to teach a person a specific skill, especially by practice."

Secondly, it is to bring or come to physical efficiency by exercise.

The word **'indispensable'** means "something that cannot be neglected."

Before we talk of neglecting the process of training, we shall define the word **'negligence'.**

'Negligence' means "carelessness or lack of proper care and attention."

It will be foolishness for someone, after receiving help from God by getting access, through insight by the Holy Ghost, into the very purpose of his existence, to jump into it without a proper training for effectiveness and efficiency.

*"He chose also David His servant, and took him from the sheepfolds, from following the ewes that had young. He brought him to shepherd Jacob His people and Israel His inheritance. So, he shepherd them according to the integrity of his heart, and guided them by the skillfulness of his hands"* (Psalm 78:70-72, NKJV)

Although you have received a divine idea from heaven, which is God's divine direction for your life, he will never put it fully in your hands for management until he has found you faithful and capable. God believes in capability and faithfulness.

Look at the divine inspiration God gave to Jethro, the father-in-law to Moses, to instruct Moses with:

*"Moreover thou shalt provide out of all the people able men, such as fear God, men of truth, hating covetousness: and place such over them, to be rulers of thousands, and rulers of fifties, and rulers of tens"* (Exodus 18:21)

You can see it very vividly here. He talked about able men first. Before he chose you for any business—secular or ministry, he has already deposited the equivalent latent potential or ability that demands a proper development for effective service disposal.

He never would have chosen David for such a sensitive position without allowing him to undergo sheep-rearing training in order to learn patience, longsuffering, meekness, love, compassion, and to develop his mind for leadership. God does not believe in your mere academic certificate. God believes in your skill, that is, your (refined) ability to handle or do a thing.

When Moses was in Egypt, he wanted to begin his divine assignment (saving and shepherding God's people) by killing an Egyptian (who was fighting with an Israelite) via his scientific and technological skill he learnt in Egypt, but God said, **"No, Moses, it cannot be possible."** And God made him to learn how to shepherd the sheep under Jethro (who became his father-in-law) for forty years in order to know how to shepherd God's people.

Perhaps you studied a course in a higher institution, and afterward you discovered your area of calling in life, you still need to go for training for your newly discovered vision. You don't just jump into it without acquiring the equivalent skill to match; you need skill.

When God decided to put Jesus in the ministry, the Master of ministries, he first made him sit under tutors before making him a Master, and he (Jesus) founded the gospel and Christianity on earth (Galatians 4:1-6). This same Jesus then trained up the twelve disciples, who later became the first leaders of the people of God after Jesus. Praise God (Mark 3:14, 15)!

To be trained is to be prepared for the great task ahead of you because you must not bring shame to the God that called you. How long we can stand the challenges of our time is a function of how well we lay our foundation. Every gigantic mansion that will ever last a long while must have a solid well-laid foundation; otherwise it will collapse with time.

Every high calling demands a high training. Excellent result is a product of excellent training. Information is a medium of communicating knowledge, while training is a way of imparting skill. Training offers practical and applicable education.

Experts in any secular field are made via training for skills and expertise. Quality training will spell out the lasting effect of your service to your generation.

Success is not in age; it is in the expertise gathered as a result of the training a man subjected himself to. Success is in what you know and are able to do with your hands easily.

The 'How' of any adventure defines its pattern. So, to be trained is to be taught a pattern of operation. A life without a pattern is an aimless life, a life void of order. The essence of order is to acquire speed for productivity. The disciples of Jesus patterned their lives and ministries after that of Jesus after they were trained by him. Read these Scriptures:

*"Now when they saw the boldness of Peter and John, and perceived that they were uneducated and untrained men, they marveled. And they realized that they had been with Jesus"* (Acts 4:13).

They were neither educated nor trained in any other area of endeavor, but they learnt what they were doing from the Lord Jesus. So the pattern of Jesus boosted their ministries.

Training offers Wisdom. Wisdom is the rightful application of foresight and experience. Training also offers experience and maturity. Remember, an office is not given to a novice. A novice is one full of assumptions. Training offers stability in any area you want to follow. To submit to a trainer is to release one's future to a thorough foundational work. A master in any field (one who knows better) trains a novice. This is done in the form of placing checks and balances, corrections and rebukes, when and where necessary. Training offers patience—a tool for overcoming discouragement at any time in the journey of life. Training helps you to be accountable.

## GOD'S UNCHANGEABLE PROGRAMME

Every man's life is divided into three major phases; and it is as follows:

1.  Growth stage
2.  Waxing or maturing (learning) stage
3.  Manifestation stage

Your destiny or purpose is a heavenly appointment. Where you were born, how you were born, and when you were born are all functions of destiny. God has been monitoring your life from when you were born till your present time. That you are alive today is because God's eyes have been on you.

Growth time is knowledge acquisition time; waxing time is a time one exercises his knowledge by practice under a trainer. It could be working with a company after your schooling to develop your skill. It could be working with a business firm or with a ministry as a pastor, evangelist, etc. in order to develop your skill. This is maturity stage.

God will not put anything in your hand to do, as a master, when you have not learned faithfulness in another man's business. Either you want to be a company owner, a Church founder or an institution owner, you have to learn the "how" of it before God can be with you in your own or give you your own. Don't be too proud to learn. Be humble (James 4:6)! You have to be a faithful steward before you can be a successful master.

Look at this:

*"And if ye have not been faithful in that which is another man's, who shall give you that which is your own"* (Luke 16:12)

God honors a faithful steward (1 Corinthians 4:2). No matter what you have passed through during your stewardship, God will pay you good again.

Look at what the Bible says:

*"Bondservant, obey in all things your master according to the flesh, not with eye service, as men pleasers, but in sincerity of heart, Fearing God. And whatever you do, do it heartily as to the Lord and not to men; knowing that of the Lord, you will receive the reward of the inheritance"* (Colossians 3: 22-24)

So as a steward under a director of a business firm, founder of a ministry, etc., do your service well because what you make happen to others, God will make happen to you.

*"Therefore, whatever you want men to do to you, do also to them, for this is the law and the prophets"* (Matthew 7:12)

Life will definitely pay you back whatever you do to people or for people. So be wise!

Let's talk about manifestation time. This is a unique time when God launches you into your own divine business. This is the period when you become a master of your own endeavor. Maybe there is no specific place for you to mature your wings in order to move toward unprecedented excellence; subject the work of your hands to mentorship. Let someone mentor you (Proverbs 15:22).

Remember, knowledge and skill acquired from training will not work much until there is divine guidance, and this guidance will not come until the time of your manifestation.

God is the only true source of real guidance for a divine success. So a manifestation time is a time of divine direction (Gen. 26:1-14). Although Moses knew how to lead God's sheep, he never ceased to take instructions from God until he finished his purpose. Read the following books of the Bible: **Exodus, Leviticus, Numbers** and **Deuteronomy**.

*"He found him in a desert land and in the waste howling wilderness; he led him about, he instructed him, he kept him as the apple of his eye"* (Deuteronomy 32:10)

When your fullness of time arrives, you become most important to God (the apple of God's eye). He leads you to your place of green or greener pasture. Though your beginning may be very small, he will lead you until you become very great.

*"He made him ride on the high places of the earth, that he might eat the increase of the field; and he made him to suck honey out the rock, and oil out of the flinty rock"* (Deuteronomy 32:13)

That is, when God is leading your life, he will bring you from a low level to a higher level of life, where you can have increase. Also, no matter how hard life is to people, he will still help you get your oil and honey from it. Life will never be miserable for you any day, any time, when God is leading and you are following.

*"Though thy beginning was small, yet thy latter end should greatly increase"* (Job 8:7)

*"But the path of the just is like the shining light that shinneth more and more unto the perfect day"* (Proverbs 4:18)

Your great height is not found in your maturing stage, but in your manifestation stage.

Let's see the three stages in the word of God:

*"And the child grew, and waxed strong in spirit; and was in the deserts till the day of his shewing unto Israel"* (Luke 1:80)

Until God counts you as fully waxed, he will never show you forth to your generation. Life will never permit you to enter into your next stage until you complete the circuit of your present stage. If you decide to show yourself forth, when your time has not come, you may not like what you may experience; and remember that God will not go with you because the move was not initiated by him.

Life is spherical in nature. It is from night to day, and then from day to night. Don't leave your desert when your day has not broken yet. And never remain in your desert when your day has broken. Work does not commence in the night but in the day.

*"Jesus answered, Are there not twelve hours in a day? If any man walks in the day, he stumbleth not, because he seeth the light of this world. But if a man walk in the night, he stumbleth, because there is no light in him"* (John 11:9-10)

*"I must work the work of him that sent me, while it is day; the night cometh, when no man can work"* (John 9:4)

Your day is your manifestation period, while your night is your maturing period. Your manifestation period is your fullness of time. Every man has his manifestation time. This is the time God will fully come to you to pick you out of your desert as he did to Jacob (Deuteronomy 32:9, 10), and say to you,

*"Arise and shine, for your light has come; for the glory of the Lord is risen upon you"* (Isaiah 60:1).

The glory of the Lord contains everything you ever need to fulfill your purpose and destiny. It contains his strength, power, grace, his presence, his wealth, etc. If your light has not come (your divine season of manifestation) and his glory has not risen upon you, you are bound to struggle because you will grope in darkness and you will surely stumble in life, having problems here and there all the time, because you are walking in your night season. May God help you in Jesus' name!

No matter how much Israel cried, God never made any move for their deliverance until their time came. No matter how much Joseph must have prayed for God to lift him out of bondage, God never did until the arrival of his time for his lifting.

*"He sent a man before them, even Joseph, who was sold for a servant: whose feet they hurt with fetters: He was laid with iron: until the time that his word came: the word of the Lord tried him. The King sent and loosed him; even the ruler of the people, and let him go free, he made him lord of his house, and ruler of all his substance: to bind his princes at his pleasure; and teach his senators wisdom"* (Psalm 105:17-20)

## THE METAMORPHOSIS OF LIFE

Life is always full of amazement. Metamorphosis is the process of change from an awkward condition or form to a glorious stage; a stage where everybody would want to identify with you.

Life is always tough at the maturing and the early beginning stages. An airplane struggles when running on the ground, trying to take off. It also experiences a little struggle when taking off until it reaches a point where it knows no struggle but is guided with the steering based on direction and compass. This is the manifestation stage. God will take you there in Jesus name!

Every man undergoes changes in life from time to time. God made it so; therefore, you can't change it. It is God's divine program.

*"To everything there is a season, and a time to every purpose under the heaven"* (Ecclesiastes 3:1)

*"Because to every purpose there is time and judgment, therefore the misery of man is great upon him. For he knoweth not that which shalt be: for who can tell him when it shall be"* (Ecclesiastes 8:6, 7)

God judges you well, when your time is come. The moment your time for a change from one level of life to another reaches its fullness, God makes sure he is on time with you and for you, no matter what tends to happen to the contrary.

You see, because man does not know his times and seasons, when it shall be, he goes about in haste, trying to move himself to the nest level, which is not in his power but in the power of God (Acts 1:6,7). A man of much haste is a man full of errors, and afterward, he blames someone else, or even God, for his own errors, which he committed with his own hands and through his own decisions (Proverbs 19:21,30).

Look at what a man who went ahead of you said in his own time:

*"If a man dies, shall he live again? All the days of my appointed time will I wait, till my change come"* (Job 14:14)

This is a clear proof that every man's change is hiding within his appointed time. So there should be no jittering. Just be doing what you are presently doing at this present time and never worry about it. If you have tried to initiate a change and it has not worked upon all your effort, just relax in God's arms, because, if God does not want you to stumble in life, he will resist your journey of life to make sure he keeps you from being destroyed or from hurrying out of your present blessing(s). I see God on your side right now. You will not fail!

In God's Kingdom, no one remains the same forever. The life of a man changes per time and the inspiration to leave a level comes when the time comes.

Although God promised Joseph a great future, he only perfected it in his own time. When your time to reign has not come, no matter how you pray and fast, and cry before God, you will never move him for anything (Job 23:13, 14).

Life is in phases: men are in sizes.

What about Joseph, a man with God's promise on his life through divine revelation? You can get the whole story in Genesis chapter forty-one. One thing I know is that no matter how life tries to toss you, God will always be on time to settle you and make sure he bring his promises to fully come to pass in your life. You will make it! No matter the journey of life you are embarking on, you are bound to follow life phase by phase. The bible says,

*"A faithful man shall abound with blessings: but he that maketh haste to be rich shall not be innocent. He that hasteth to be rich hath an evil eye, and considereth not that poverty shall come upon him"* (Proverbs 28:20, 22)

Why men struggle vainly in life is because they never allow God to move them through the phases of life. Remember, when the children of Israel were going to the land of Canaan, God followed and led them with a pillar of cloud by the day and a pillar of fire by night.

When you read the passages carefully, you will discover that they never moved forward until the pillar of cloud in the day time and the pillar of fire by night moved ahead of them alternatively (Exodus 13:21-22; Numbers 9:15-23; 10:33). These pillars were both meant to give them protection and direction respectively in their journey. So, when you hurry in life, you are bound to either make mistakes or fall into evil, because God never hurries.

Look at God's laid-down covenant program for your day-to-day success:

*"But the path of the just is as a shining light, that shineth more and more unto the perfect day"* (Proverbs 4:18)

So if you keep struggling and keep worrying, you are only reducing your life span.

The following are the signs of divine promotion to the next phase in life:

1. Divine inspiration or insight: divine insight lunches you into your next phase in life.

Where you can't see, you can't reach. If God wants to increase your border, he will do it by giving you insight into what next to do and give you a divine idea on how to do it. This is what brings breakthroughs, when God involves himself in helping you to do it.

When God is not with you in any pursuit, life will wage war with you; but when he is with you, you have no choice but to prosper (Deuteronomy 2:7), and every hindrance will give way for you (Psalm

114:1-8), because the achievement of your purpose in life will come phase by phase, and these phases are subject to time (Job 14:14).

Let's look at these Scriptures:

*"And I will send hornets before thee, which shall drive out the Hivites, the Canaanites, and the Hittites, from before thee. I will not drive them out from thee in one year; lest the land before thee become desolate, and the beast of the field multiply against thee. By little and little I will drive them out from before thee, until thou be increased . . ."* (Exodus 23:28-30)

This promise shows that God does not promote automatically from level one to ten, or else, you will be destroyed, not being able to handle the promotion. He knows your ability and strength. He knows what to put into your hands from time to time.

God has boundaries attached to your destiny phase by phase. He removes them from time to time to allow your increase. He never hurries. So you need patience, which is defined as the ability to understand the duties and benefits of your present time. Promotion comes when you are overdue for your present stage.

2. The next sign is that you will easily find human help.
3. Open doors of financial provision
4. Divine provision of materials needed for the achievement of your divine idea or insight received.
5. Your workers, or those that will help you, will possess a willing heart that is stirred up by God.
6. Things will work out easily for you.
7. All oppositions will bow out of the way for you.
8. God's hand will be with you and on you for success.
9. And, also, everything will be excellent in the eyes of men and of God.

Read the story of Nehemiah and Ezra (Ezra 7, 8; and throughout the book of Nehemiah). Praise the Lord! I see God's hand resting on you from today in Jesus' name!

The truth is that there is a season when you are bound to pass through life's battles. Although people don't want to hear this, it does not change the agenda of destiny. Everyone who is at the top today has a story or stories to tell the world, even if their parents handed over wealth to them.

Let's see the statement King David made concerning the journey of Israel from one phase to the other via time:

*"For thou, O God, hast proved us: thou hast tried us, as silver is tried. Thou broughtest us into the net; thou laidst affliction upon our loins. Thou hast caused men to ride over our heads; we went through fire and through water: but thou broughtest us out into a wealthy place"* (Psalm 66:10-12)

God is the God of phase and time. He never changes. He is the same yesterday, today and forever (Malachi 3:6). You will get to your wealthy place in Jesus' name. Life will definitely pass you through processes before ever you become what you really desire.

Look at this:

*"As the fining pot for silver and the furnace for gold; so is a man to his praise."* (Proverbs 27:21)

So, if you want to shine like gold, expect fire; if you want to shine like silver, expect the fining pot.

Many people want the praise of life, but never want to pass through life experiences. Similarly, people like hearing the stories behind others' success but would never want to go through any kind of life's challenge.

The only possible road to good and astounding success is Psalm 66:10-12. There is no other shortcut. Any other shortcut will definitely cut you down. So be careful! I see God helping you to your wealthy place.

You may ask, "How long will it be?" It is God that will determine that, and not man (Acts 1:7). All you need is patience. That's all.

*"Blessed is the man that endureth temptation: for when he is tried, he shall receive the crown of life, which he hath promised to them that love him"* (*James 1:12*)

107

*"But let endurance and steadfastness and patience have full play and do a thorough work, so that you may be (people) perfectly and fully developed (with no defects, lacking in nothing"* (James 1:4, AMP)

Patience will convey you to your wealthy place with a refined personality.

# THE PURSUIT OF INFORMATION

What is information? This is a fact discovered or received from a source about a particular matter. It is equally called knowledge.

A man without positive information about what he is pursuing in life will definitely fall into disaster. Information is light, while ignorance is darkness. If you are not informed, you will be totally lost in life. In fact, I have no better language to describe your state when you are not informed in life.

How can you just jump into doing a particular thing you don't have any idea of? Information offers you the knowledge of a thing. It makes you to be up to date in life.

There are two types of information. We have creative information and synthetic information. There are also two kinds of information: specific information and generalized information.

Let me begin by explaining them singularly.

**Types of information**

1.  Creative Information: this is a type of information that comes through your sixth sense by the process of creative thinking, which comes as a mental picture by the power of imagination. In fact, it is divine information from God called inspiration.

*"Great men are not always wise: neither do the aged understand judgment. But there is a spirit in man: and the inspiration of the Almighty giveth them understanding"* (Job 32:9, 8)

*"But the comforter, which is the Holy Ghost, whom the Father will send in my name, he shall teach you all things . . ."* (John 14:26)

*"But the anointing which ye have received of him abideth in you, and ye need not that any man teach you: but as the same anointing teacheth you all things and is no lie, and even as it hath taught you, ye shall abide in him"* (John 2:27)

2.  Synthetic Information: this is information that is gotten from institutions, books, tapes, seminars, conferences, research, media, Internet, etc. It is a booster which helps a great deal to illuminate you for better understanding of the creative information you received; hence, it is an elucidator.

This is the kind of information that brought about the initiation of this topic—the pursuit of information. You need to broaden your mentality on the ideas you are trying to bring to reality.

## Kinds of Information

1.  General information: this is the kind of information that people try to gather, and which can never be put to use for positive or possible dividends. To pursue this kind of information is a real waste of time. You can never be Mr. "Know-all." It will be good for you to pursue the information that concerns your purpose for existence, and make use of the expertise of others where necessary. This will keep you focused and establish your going.
2.  Specific knowledge/information: this is known as synthetic information based on specific purpose.

To maximize your productivity in life at any period of time, pursue after profitable information. There are many things within your assignment not yet done, waiting for your humble attention. Don't disappoint them.

Nothing is as good as reading. Even if you have attained a level of PhD in your area of pursuit and other helpful courses, it is not a criterion to stop reading. To stop reading is the beginning of mental decadence.

Nothing is as worse as mental decadence in life. Your value is attached to your mind. How you think, talk or behave is a product of information gathered.

The mind is the engine of a man's life, while information is the fuel that makes it work properly. Every man's life is equal to his mind's capacity to deliver. Your level in life is determined and measured by the information you have gathered in your life from stage to stage. How much you know about what you are ever doing is a function of your related knowledge base. If you know more, you will do more, and do it even better. Don't be static in knowledge. Look for the best ways to do whatever you are doing, either by contacting God for divine information for the expansion of your God-given idea that you are executing, or by going for more elucidating synthetic information.

*"And be not conformed to this world: but be ye transformed by the renewing of your mind . . . "* (Romans 12:2)

The Bible says that as a man thinks in his heart, so is he (Proverbs 23:7b). Transformation, therefore, begins in the mind. To be transformed is to change from one form to a more preferred form in life. You will never understand life beyond your knowledge base. If anybody will ever change from his or her present stage to a higher one, from third-world class to the class of the civilized (from mediocrity to excellence), insight or light, through higher information that breeds transformation, is the answer.

Changes in social and financial status come via increasing your information bank, either divinely or synthetically. Don't remain in one point forever. Don't be a local champion. Transformation begins between your two ears and your two eyes. Go for higher learning. Expand your brain.

## Sources of information

1. The Bible: this reveals the secrets for success and prosperity in whatever God commanded you to do. It also offers guidance from wrong steps and guidance into right paths of life (Acts 2:28; Joshua 1:8; Psalm 1:1-3). It is God's manual for life and endeavors.

## Why you must study the Bible

a. To understand the secrets of your make-up spiritually and to know your spiritual potentials in the likeness of God (1 John 4:17; Psalm 82:6;

2 Peter 1:4). b. To know the nature of the covenants that is binding you and God: the covenant terms, and your covenant responsibilities in order to achieve your covenant blessings in Christ Jesus (Deuteronomy 7:7-15). c. To know how to locate your purpose for existing and how to fulfill it in line with God's order. (Proverbs 19:21; 20:24; Jeremiah 10:23; Joshua 1:8). d. To know your office here on earth as regards to your relationship with heaven, hell and earth in terms of spiritual political leadership(Isaiah 45:12; Psalm 8:4-8; Genesis 1:26; Luke 10:18,19,20). e. To know your heavenly financial back-up and how to connect yourself to it (Philippians 4:19; Romans 8:32; 2 Peter 1:3). f. To know the position that God has in your business or the work of your hand and your destiny (John 15:4-7). g. To discover the nothingness of Satan and his kingdom based on his defeat on the Cross (John 12:31). h. To find out your right, as a heavenly citizen, in relation to the Godhead, angels and the earth. (Isaiah 45:12; Genesis 1:26). God is your Father, Jesus is your Lord, the Holy Spirit is your helper, the angels are your servants, and you are in charge on the earth. i. To know more about the kingdom you belong to and j. To know how to grow spiritually and mentally; and even the Godhead based on their responsibilities respectively toward you.

2.   The compilation of people's thoughts—books, tapes and periodicals

3.   Travelling for discovery (Proverbs 24:30-34)

3.   Seminars and conferences

4.   Church: it is the place of divine and social institution.

5.   Positive relationship: relating with learned people that have right information, success-oriented people, people of life-beaming visions and high expectations, people who never see failure as it is, but as a product of wrong button(s) that was/were pressed (Proverbs 13:20).

6.   Divine inspirations (Job 32:8): this is the function of the fear of the Lord.

7.   Institutions for higher learning

Remember this: *"And wisdom and knowledge shall be the stability of thy times, and strength of salvation: the fear of the Lord is his treasure"* (Isaiah 33:6)!

## The effects of information

Here, we are going to talk about the effects of both divine and human information.

1. It leads to witty inventions (Proverbs 8: 12; Ecclesiastes 7: 29)
2. It leads to discoveries (Ecclesiastes 7:25; Proverbs 2:1-9; Proverbs 24:30-34)
3. It helps you to locate directions whenever you are lost out in any matter (Ecclesiastes 10:10)
4. It leads in the way of righteousness (Proverbs 8:12, 20)
5. It leads to profitable labor (1 Tim. 4:15)
6. It leads to mighty works (Mark 6:2)
7. It makes your face bright all the time always smiling, knowing what to do at all time, and how to get what you want, never worrying (Ecclesiastes 8:1)
8. It leads to creativity (Exodus 28:3; 31:6; 35:10-19, 25, 26; 36:1, 2, 8)
9. It offers boldness and confidence in whatever a man is doing
10. It eliminates assumption
11. It gives you assurance of having the desired results
12. It makes you outstanding in your work and among the crowd
13. It brings about honor and glory (Ecclesiastes 2:13)
14. It gives birth to excellence in life
15. It puts you ahead of the people within your area of endeavor
16. It makes you see farther and deeper than others (Ecclesiastes 2:14)
17. It offers you dominion in your area of life
18. Once you get direction in what to do about a matter and how to do it, it will make you do all things well (Mark 7:31-37)
18. It offers you value in life. How effectively your mind can deliver answers to your generation determines your worth to people
19. When information begins to deliver results into your hands, you begin to command the respect of people
20. It eliminates the fear of mistake from your mind concerning an adventure

In conclusion, an ignorant man gets the opposite of everything we have just mentioned so far.

*"Also, that the soul be without knowledge, it is not good . . ."* (Proverbs 19:2a)

Among all these sources of information, the only one that breaks the backbone of worry over a particular matter is inspiration; and this can only come from God through the Holy Spirit. Nevertheless, the best time to get inspiration is the earliest time of the day and the night seasons.

*"Day unto day uttereth speech and night unto night showeth knowledge"* (Psalm 19:2)

*". . . He wakeneth morning by morning, he wakeneth my ear to hear as the learned"* (Isaiah. 50:4b)

So, as you use your night and early morning seasons well, may the Father of our Lord Jesus Christ deliver ideas for breakthroughs into your hand in Jesus' mighty name! Amen.

# CHAPTER EIGHT

## THE RELEVANCE OF FAITH IN THE PURSUIT OF DESTINY

BEFORE ANYTHING CAN BE relevant, it must be a thing that one cannot do without. In life, everybody has a kind of faith in him or her. Every action is a product of what a man believes. No man takes any convincing step in life without having faith in what he is going to do. Faith is the basis of everything anyone does in life. Faith is a determinant factor in the world of success. Until you fully believe that what you are going for in life is achievable or can be done, you can never begin its journey. So, faith is a relevant factor for life to be enviable and enjoying.

Let's look at Hebrews 11:2, 7, and 9: *"For by faith the elders obtained a good report. By faith Noah, being warned of God of things not seen as yet, moved with fear, prepared an ark to the saving of his house . . . By faith Abraham, when he was called to go out into a place, which he should after receive for an inheritance, obeyed; and he went out, not knowing whither he went. By faith he sojourned in the land of promise, as in a strange country, dwelling in tabernacles with Isaac and Jacob, the heirs with him of the same promise"* (Hebrews 11:2,7,9).

The impossible is only achievable by the instrumentality of faith. Nothing is too hard when faith is in place. Every great mountain is waiting for the arrival of your faith in God. From stage to stage, there are always impossible doors to every next level in life, which are waiting for the key of faith, which is released by the instruction(s) of God.

The men we just read about in the previous verses were men that heard God's voice, and saw the revelation of God concerning the future. These men believed God for what he told them.

In one of the previous chapters, we talked about how God speaks to us. And one of those ways is through divine revelation, either by trance or dream at sleep time (Numbers 24:16; Job 33:14-18).

What could have been the story of those men we read about, if they had no faith in God for what he told them? But thank God that they believed in him and God confirmed his word to them because,

*". . . Without faith it is impossible to please Him: for he that cometh to God must believed that He is, and that He is a rewarder of them that diligently seek Him"* (Hebrews 11:6)

The angel that spoke to Mary, the mother of Jesus, said to her,

*". . . Blessed is she that believe: for there shall be a performance of those things which were told her from the Lord"* (Luke 1:45)

Also, one of the twelve disciples also said, **". . . He that believeth not God hath made him a liar" (1 John 5:10b).**

Let's look at what happened to Zechariah, the father of John the Baptist, so we can fully understand the purpose of the very topic we are treating now.

*"And there appeared unto him an angel of the Lord standing on the right side of the altar of incense. And when Zacharias saw him, he was troubled, and fear fell upon him. But the angel said unto him, Fear not, Zacharias: for thy prayer is heard; and thy wife Elisabeth shall bear thee a son, and thou shalt call his name John . . . And Zacharias said unto the angel, Whereby shall I know this? For I am an old man, and my wife well stricken in years. And the angel answering said unto him, I am Gabriel that stand in the presence of God; and am sent to speak unto thee, and to shew thee these glad tidings. And behold, thou shalt be dumb, and not able to speak*

*until the day that these things shall be performed, because thou believest not my word, which shall be fulfilled in their season"* (Luke 1:11-20)

Anytime you doubt God when He speaks to you, either by revelation or by rhema, you provoke God to wrath. Faith is what brings about the promises of God into reality. It is impossible for God to lie or for Him to change His Word, which He has already declared to either a country or an individual.

## The faithfulness of God towards his word

Let us see God's faithfulness towards his word through the following Scriptures:

*"God is not a man, that he should lie; neither the son of man, that he should repent: hath he said, and shall he not do it? Or hath he spoken and shall he not make it good"* (Numbers 23:19)

*"Then said the Lord unto me, Thou hast well seen: for I will hasten my word to perform it"* (Jeremiah 1:12)

*"Nevertheless my lovingkindness will I not utterly take from him, nor suffer my faithfulness to fail. My covenant will I not break, nor alter the thing that is gone out of my mouth"* (Psalm 89:33, 34)

*"Can a woman forget her sucking child, that she should not have compassion on the son of her womb? Yea, they may forget, yet will I not forget thee"* (Isaiah 49:15)

*"Faithful is he that calleth you, who also will do it"* (I Thessalonians 5:24)

*"Being confident of this very thing, that he which hath begun a good work in you will perform it until the day of Jesus Christ"* (Philippians 1:6)

*"Son of man, what is that proverb that ye have in the land of Israel, saying, The days are prolonged, and every vision faileth? Tell them therefore, thus saith the Lord God: I will make this proverb to cease, and they shall no more use it as a proverb in Israel; but say unto them, The days are at hand, and the effect of every vision. For there shall be no more any vain vision nor flattering divination within the house of Israel. For I am the Lord: I*

*will speak, and the word that I shall speak shall come to pass; it shall be no more prolonged: for in your days, O rebellious house, will I say the word, and will perform it, saith the Lord God"* (Ezekiel 12:22-25)

*"And being not weak in faith, he considered not his own body now dead, when he was about an hundred years old, neither yet the deadness of Sarah's womb. He staggered not at the promise of God through unbelief; but was strong in faith, giving glory to God; and being fully persuaded that, what he had promised, He was able also to perform"* (Romans 4:19-21)

*"The Lord is not slack concerning his promise, as some men count slackness"* (2 Peter 3:9a)

*". . . with whom there is no variableness, neither shadow of turning"* (James 1:17)

*"For I am the Lord, I change not"* (Malachi 3:6a)

*"And the Lord, he it is that doth go before thee; he will be with thee, he will not fail thee, neither forsake thee: fear not, neither be dismayed"* (Deuteronomy 31:8)

Now, with all these Scriptures, has faith jumped up on your inside? I guess so. You can now see that God will make sure and make haste to fulfill his word before your eyes. He will definitely show you his faithfulness in Jesus' mighty name!

## WHAT FAITH IS

Faith is not an assumption. It is not abstract. It is not jumping in the dark. It is walking in the light of divine insight or the revelation of God's word to you concerning a matter (for positive results in the area of the matter). Every instruction God gives you carries the equivalent faith for possible accomplishment.

Faith is placing confidence in God and his word, which you heard or received.

*"In whom we have boldness and access with confidence through faith in Him"* (Ephesians 3:12)

Faith, in Greek word, simply is **'Pisteuo',** which also means to be persuaded of.

*"For this reason I also suffer these things; nevertheless I am not ashamed, for I know whom I have believed and am persuaded that he is able to keep what I have committed unto him until that day"* (2 Timothy 1:12)

It also means to have conviction for things that we hope for. It is the evidence of things not seen (Hebrews 11:1). It is the real interpretation of negative matters according to their divine realities, based on the persuasion in our mind.

*". . . who quickeneth the dead, and calleth those things which be not, as though they were"* (Romans 4:17b)

Faith is an absolute dependence upon the word of God and his Son, Jesus Christ.

*"The centurion answered and said, Lord, I am not worthy that thou shouldest come under my roof, but speak the word only, and my servant shall be healed"* (Matthew 8:8)

Faith is trusting wholly and unreservedly in the faithfulness of God. Remember the three Hebrew boys (Daniel 3:4-30). Faith is being sure that the word that God has spoken to you shall come to pass.

*"But after long abstinence Paul stood forth in the midst of them, and said, Sirs, ye should have hearkened unto me, and not have loosed from Crete, and to have gained this harm and loss. And now I exhort you to be of good cheer: for there shall be no loss of any man's life among you, but of the ship. For there stood by me this night the angel of God, whose I am, and whom I serve, saying, Fear not, Paul; thou must be brought before Caesar: and lo, God hath given thee all them that stand with thee. Wherefore, sirs, be of good cheer: for I believe God that it shall be even as it was told me"* (Acts 27:21-22)

Faith is the cooperation between the attribute of God and the restored faculty of man, whereby both can bring into existence things that are not seen.

*"And the Lord said unto Moses, Wherefore criest thou unto me? Speak unto the children of Israel that they go forward: but lift thou up thy rod, and*

*stretch out thine hand over the sea, and divide it: and the children of Israel shall go on dry ground through the midst of the sea. And Moses stretched out his hand over the sea; and the Lord caused the sea to go back by a strong east wind all that night, and made the sea dry land, and the waters were divided. And the children of Israel went into the midst of the sea upon the dry ground: and the waters were a wall unto them on their right hand, and on their left . . ."* (Exodus 14:15; 16, 21, 11, 26-30)

This is faith-walk between God and man. The following scriptures contain more examples for this later definition of faith (1 Kings 17:8-16; 2 Kings 3:10-25).

Faith is the act of man that compels the move of God's hand.

*"And again he entered into Capernaum after some days; and it was noised that he was in the house. And straight way many were gathered, insomuch that there was no room to receive them, no, not so much as about the door: and he preached the word to them. And they come unto him, bringing one sick of the palsy, Which was borne of four,. And when they could not come nigh unto him for the press, they uncovered the roof where he was: and when they had broken it up, they let them the bed wherein the sick of the palsy lay. When Jesus saw their faith, he said unto the sick of the palsy, son, thy sins be forgiven thee . . . I say unto thee, Arise, and take up thy bed, and go thy way into thine house. And immediately he arose, took up the bed, and went forth before them all: insomuch that they were all amazed, and glorified God, saying, We never saw it on this fashion"* (Mark 2:1-5,11,12)

*"And a certain woman, which had an issue of blood twelve years, and had suffered many things of many physicians and had spent all that she had, and was nothing better, but rather grew worse, when she had heard of Jesus, came in the press behind, and touched his garment. For she said, if I may touch but his clothes, I shall be whole. And straightway the fountain of her blood was dried up; and she felt in her body that she was healed of that plague. And Jesus immediately knowing that virtue has gone out of him, turned him about in the press, and said, Who touched my clothes? And his disciples said unto him, thou seest the multitude thronging thee, and sayest thou, Who touched me? And he looked round about to see her that had done this thing. But the woman fearing and trembling, knowing what was*

*done in her, came and knelt down before him, and told him all the truth. And he said unto her, Daughter, thy faith hath made thee whole, go in peace, and be whole of thy plague"* (Mark 5:25-34)

Faith attracts miracle, which are events that exceed the known laws of nature and science.

*"By faith, Enoch was translated that he should not see death; and was not found, because God has translated him: for before his translation he had this testimony, that he please God"* (Hebrews 11:5)

Faith is the creative force for divine works.

*"Through faith we understand that the worlds were framed by the word of God, so that things which are seen were not made of things which do appear"* (Hebrews 11:3)

Faith is trust in the unseen future through divine revelation from God.

*"By faith Abraham, when he was called to go out into a place which he should after receive for an inheritance, obeyed; and he went out, not knowing whither he went. By faith he sojourned in the land of promise, as in a strange country, dwelling in tabernacles with Isaac and Jacob, the heirs with him of the same promise. For he looked for a city, which hath foundation, whose builder and maker is God"* (Hebrews 11: 8-10)

Faith is seeing things that are invisible and both declaring them and working them out or acting as if it is already a reality (Exodus 12:1-30; Job 3:7-17; 6: 1, 20).

Faith is having confidence that something will come to pass as God has revealed it to you (Hebrews11:20-31).

Faith is enduring the present temporal affliction or pain by the strength of the insight gained into a better future.

*"Looking unto Jesus the author and finisher of our faith; who for the joy that was set before him endured the cross, despising the shame, and is set down at he right hand of the throne of God"* (Hebrews 12:2)

Faith is the active way of bringing spiritual realities into existence physically. It is walking in the light of divine idea(s) to bring into place things beyond the natural. Hence it is the gap in which a man can stand to attract things from the supernatural realm into the natural realm, and the end result is called 'Miracle'.

Faith is hearing God and declaring his word over a situation to cause a change to take place (2 Kings 7:1-20).

Faith is obeying the instructions of God in order to connect oneself to his covenant blessings (Deuteronomy 28:1-14). Obedience is the stronghold of faith. Faith can only be expressed through willful obedience.

Faith is the livelihood of the just. It is the edible spiritual substance with which the just are fed, and it is only obtained through the word of God.

*"Now the just shall live by faith . . ."* (Hebrews 10:38a)

*"And he humbled thee, and suffered thee to hunger, and fed thee with manna, which thou knewest not, neither did thy fathers know; that he might make thee know that man doth not live by bread only, but by every word that proceedeth out of the mouth of the Lord doth man live"* (Deuteronomy 8:3)

Faith is seeing where God is taking you to in life and preparing yourself for it (taking steps toward it).

*"By faith Noah, being warned of God of things not seen as yet, moved with fear, prepared an ark to the saving of his house; by the which he condemned the world, and became heir of the righteousness which is by faith"* (Hebrews 11:7)

Noah saw that God wanted to take him out from among the wicked generation of the people in the world at that time, and to start a new generation on earth, after condemning the people in it so he prepared himself toward it by building an ark to save his family.

Preparation is the highest proof of faith. To really show that you believe what God has told you concerning your future, you have to prepare for it, or else the floods of life will overtake you. May God help you out in the name of Jesus!

Faith is the spiritual password that opens up the heavens for the downpour of things desired or hoped for.

*"And we desire that every one of you do shew the same diligence to the full assurance of hope unto the end: that ye be not slothful, but followers of them who through faith and patience inherit the promise"* (Hebrews 6:11, 12)

Faith is the guarantee for an answered prayer. It is the confidence that our prayers are heard when we meet the demands of His will in prayer.

*"Therefore I say unto you, what things so ever ye desire, when ye pray, believe that ye receive them, and ye shall have them"* (Mark 11:24)

*"And this is the confidence that if we ask any thing according to his will, he heareth us. And if we know that he heareth us, whatsoever we ask, we know that we have the petitions that we desire of him"* (1 John 5:14-15)

Now you can see the true definitions of faith, and that it is an active force that compels a man to do the unusual and the unnatural to allow for the equivalent unusual happenings or occurrences. It is parallel to the philosophies and traditions of men. It does not agree with human reasoning. A man of faith is actually a mad man in the eyes of the world because; he does not behave nor think like them. I see this kind of faith come alive in you in the name of Jesus.

**How Faith Comes**

Before we talk about how faith comes, let me tell you about the two kinds of faith.

We have the passive faith and the active faith. The passive faith is the kind of faith that is birthed in you when you receive the understanding of God's word through men's preaching. This is called hope (you just believe that something is possible, but you do not yet have the persuasion to go for it) and you will remain in this level, when you have not started hearing the voice of God, which produces an active faith.

Passive faith does not produce action. It only ends in giving you understanding. It comes via logos—the written word of God. It contains no compulsive force to make you take steps.

For example, you can believe that God can do a thing but may not be able to move God into action in your favor. This kind of faith can be easily impeded by fear. It is impotent. It is called faith at a distance. You can believe that God can heal the lame all because you heard it from a man of God, but may not be able to act on the same for your lameness to be healed, for it has no equivalent force for application.

The book of James calls it **"dead faith"** because it has no force that produces work. Even when you try to conjure this kind of faith for action through mental assent, because it has no life in it, it will still not produce the desired result, except the Holy Spirit cause you to brood over this acquired knowledge in your mental region to cause inspiration and move it from your conscious mind to your subconscious mind by giving life to the written word and causes it to become rhema.

*". . . For the letter killeth, but the Spirit giveth life"* (2 Corinthians 3:6b)

This kind of faith that comes via the word being preached by the minister as logos ends in our hearts and mouth, but does not gain trigger ability.

*"But what saith it? The word is nigh thee, even in thy mouth, and in thy heart: that is, the word of faith, which we preach"* (Romans 10:8)

On the other hand, the active kind of faith has a spirit behind it that makes you declare it out or act immediately on it; although it can be hindered by doubt if allowed to undergo mental analysis and delay; except it is acted upon immediately.

*"We having the same spirit of faith, according as it is written, I believe, and therefore have I spoken; we also believe and therefore speak"* (2 Corinthians 4:13)

When you have faith by the Holy Ghost, it makes you an active believer in the Lord.

*"And the Spirit entered into me when he spake unto me, and set me upon my feet, as I heard him that spake unto me"* (Ezekiel 2:2)

This kind of faith comes via the hearing ear.

*"Therefore do not fear them. For there is nothing covered that will not be revealed, and hidden that will not be known. Whatever I tell you in the dark, speak in the light; and what you hear in the ear, preach on the housetops"* (Matthew 10:26, 27)

*"But blessed are your eyes, for they see: and your ears, for they hear"* (Matthew 13:16)

*"So then faith cometh by hearing, and hearing by the word of God"* (Romans 10:17)

All the people mentioned in Hebrews chapter eleven that obtained good reports as the exploits of their faith were people that heard God or had the revelation of God.

Some of them had their results by gaining conviction through meditating on the preceding testimonies heard concerning God's dealings with the Israelites, e.g. the harlot in Jericho, who saved the lives of the two spies.

This is the only possible means of translating a passive faith into an active faith, that is, from head knowledge to your spirit man. I mean meditating on gained knowledge until it causes an illumination in your heart and moves you into action by the Holy Ghost.

*"We have also a more sure word of prophecy; whereunto ye do well that ye take heed, as unto a light that shineth in a dark place, until the day dawn, and the day star arise in your hearts"* (2 Peter. 1:19)

Day dawning means divine understanding by the inspiration of God, while the day-star-arising means faith arising in your hearts for action.

Jesus is the author and the finisher of this kind of faith (Hebrews 12:2a), and it comes as a rhema (God's voice) from God.

When this kind of faith comes, you are neither far from having the miraculous (from achieving the unusual or supernatural occurrence), because it will always move the hand of God.

This very kind of faith is always warm and vital because it lives; it throbs our heart with undeniable excitement, and its power is absolutely irresistible. When God's kind of faith, which is a gift from the Holy Ghost (1 Corinthians 12:4,9a), comes into your heart concerning a matter that is causing you worry or anxiety, the storm dies down and a great calm follows with a deep settled peace in the soul. The only noise you will eventually hear will be the murmured voice of thanksgiving and praise and a shout of halleluiah, springing up from your inside.

To crown up this vital issue, all I am saying is this: when God speaks to you by revelation, telling you what your future entails and showing you the kind of relevance your existing personality carries towards your generation, a certain lively force will be birthed in you, and this lively force is called "faith", which will help you to achieve that enviable future. Hope is entwined with this faith.

This faith comes with joy unspeakable and makes you very optimistic. This is what makes a man gratefully appreciate the opportunity given him to appear visibly on the surface of this planet earth, a place of potential display for the benefit of both present and future generations.

Nevertheless, be careful not to let the word that God spoke to you to slip out of your mind; because if you forget the word of God that came to you concerning a matter, the equivalent faith dies in your heart, and you become vulnerable to sorrow, worry, anxiety, bitterness, etc. You will not be trapped in such in Jesus' mighty name!

**Faith And Facts**

I want to differentiate faith from fact in this sub-topic.

Faith comes through divine revelation, while fact is the true appearance of a thing, or physical reality.

So the first is "revelation knowledge faith", while the latter is called "sense knowledge faith".

Revelation knowledge faith, either via rhema or illumination of logos, is gained through an insight into God's word; while a sense knowledge faith is based on the five senses—smelling, hearing, seeing, feeling and tasting. These are the regions where doubt exists against the revelation knowledge faith.

Fact is the physical evidence that the devil uses to pass his verdicts, while faith is the spiritual or scriptural evidence that God uses to pass his verdicts.

Evidence is the information that gives a story a reason for believing. It is a proof that what you want is obtainable, or a divine proof that nullifies the wiles of the devil. It is the armour of God for obtaining victory over demonic operations.

*"Put on the whole armour of God, that ye may be able to stand against the wiles of the devil"* (Ephesians 6:11).

The word "whiles" means "lies", and these lies represent the physical appearance of a thing; and this thing is called "fact". So **"Fight the good fight of faith . . ." (1 Timothy 6:12).**

The fight of faith is the battle of words. That is, speaking the word of God concerning a matter against the physical appearance of the same matter. It is also challenging your situation with the revealed truth of God's word.

Faith is like a passbook that stands as evidence, which gives you access to your divine provision in heavenly places. Once you present it before God, the devil (who may stand against your approach to God for the release of health, finance, forgiveness, the prosperity of the work of your hands, etc, which are your covenant right or provision) bows out of the way for you because no one doubts proofs.

Our belief in facts reveals our ignorance of the truth (God's word) that conveys faith for victory (1 John 5:4).

Truth (faith) frees us from the yokes that our belief on facts brought us into.

*"And ye shall know the truth, and the truth shall make you free"* (John 8:32)

Fact is governed by our physical sight, while faith is governed by our insight gained from God's word.

*"For we walk by faith, not by sight"* (2 Corinthians 5:7)

Those who walk by sight can never operate in active faith. This group of people is easily moved by what they see, what they hear from common men, and what they feel.

The Bible says,

*"God is our refuge and strength, a very present help in trouble. Therefore will not we fear, though the earth be removed, and though the mountains be carried into the midst of the sea; though the waters thereof roar and be troubled, though the mountains shake with the swelling thereof"* (Psalm 46:1-3)

This is the statement of a man called David the king, who made God his backbone. So whom will you believe? If you believe God, He will show you His power (Isaiah 53:1); but if you believe the devil for his facts, you enter into bondage.

You will not be caught by Satan in Jesus' mighty name! Amen.

## THE WORKABLE FAITH

*"You believe that there is one God. You do well. Even the demons believe and tremble! But do you want to know, O foolish man, that faith without works is dead? Was not Abraham our father justified by works when he offered Isaac his son on the altar? Do you see that faith was working together with his works, and by works, faith was made perfect? You see, then, that a man is justified by works, and not by faith only. For as the body without the spirit is dead, so faith without works is dead also"* (James 2:19-22, 24, 26, N.K.J.V)

Jesus said, *"It is the Spirit that quickeneth; the words that I speak unto you, they are spirit, and they are life"* (John 6:63).

When the word of God comes to you personally, this word of God carries life and spirit. This kind of word conveys into you a living faith, which in turn finds practical expressions through your mouth and your actions. These actions prove your faith workable.

A workable faith is the faith that produces results any day, any time and at any place.

The initial scriptures under this very sub-topic tell us that it is works that make faith a perfect subject or substance. When you are not doing anything to show that you believe the word of God that comes to you at a particular time or to give your faith an expression for good report or undeniable result, your faith is termed dead.

How do you express your faith to make it a workable faith and to yield results? To provide an answer to this stimulating question, we shall look at the following operational steps:

1.   Believing God's word: faith begins its journey in the heart from the point of belief.

*"For with the heart man believeth unto righteousness . . ."* (Romans 10:10a)

Reasoning with God and His word causes an illumination in your heart, which brings you to a point of believing and eventually leading you into action.

To add to what I said earlier on, faith is discovering what to do, through God's word, to get a desired end in times of trouble. It begins by gaining insight into God's word for an answer, and by understanding what to do to solve a problem as soon as you hear from God concerning any matter.

Faith also is seeing the end of a thing before beginning the journey. It is an illumination of scripture(s) in your heart, causing faith to rise from your inside like the morning sun. It imparts courage and divine energy for a successful accomplishment. It is an understanding gained through the knowledge of God's word.

*"The entrance of thy words giveth light; it giveth understanding unto the simple"* (Psalm. 119:130)

When faith comes alive in your heart, every doubt dissolves in you; but any further delay can cause doubt to grow like weeds under your newly germinated faith, and this can render your faith impotent or unproductive.

Faith produces in you a positive mental attitude, and makes you always talk positively, no matter what you see, hear or feel.

2. Confessing God's word: for faith to work, it has to move from the believing stage to the confession stage. The power of faith is being conveyed through confession—verbal expression (giving voice to your faith).

*"How forcible are right words . . ."* (Job 6:25)

*"A man hath joy by the answer of his mouth: and a word spoken in due season, how good it is"* (Proverbs 15:23)

*". . . And with the mouth confession is made unto salvation"* (Romans 10:10b)

So, if you believe what God told you, say it.

*"We having the same spirit of faith, according as it is written, I believed and therefore have I spoken; we also believe, and therefore speak"* (2 Corinthians 4:13)

Speaking the word of God is one of the ways to bring into physical reality the things that God has revealed or spoken to you.

No matter what your present time seems to be, confess your way out of it. Abraham (formally Abram) began to bear Abraham (the father of many nations), even when he had no child. And this attitude made him become the father of many nations. His wife also did the same, changing her name from Sarai to Sarah.

Joseph made his brethren know that he was born to be king, when God revealed it to him. This also changed his perspective over his condition when he found himself as a slave in Egypt and in the prison as a prisoner. At last the word of God came through in his life.

Why must you confess God's word?

1.   Through confession, you can give God an assignment by committing Him to confirm what you said.

*"Say unto them, as truly as I live, saith the Lord, as ye have spoken in mine ears, so will I do to you"* (Numbers 14:28)

2.   God's angels attend to it to produce what you say.

*"Bless the Lord, ye his angels, that excel in strength, that do his commandments, hearkening unto the voice of his word"* (Psalm. 103:20)

3.   You are justified by your statement.

*"For by thy words thou shalt be justified, and by thy words thou shalt be condemned"* (Matthew 12:37)

*". . . declare thou, that thou mayest be justified"* (Isaiah 43:26)

4.   God confirms the word (of God that you spoke) with signs following.

*". . . the Lord working with them, and confirming the word with signs following"* (Mark 16:20)

Every word you speak on this wise will be creative. It will cause the fact on ground to change to your expectation. And this will happen when God confirms your word.

There was a young man, who was thirsty and rushed into the science laboratory in their school to look for water. He found a bottle of water and then drank from it. After a while, someone saw him, rushed him, and told him that the bottle contains an acidic liquid, which he did not check out because he was so thirsty. When they checked it out with a litmus paper, it proved acidic.

Fear was about entering the young man, but all of a sudden, the word of God came to him, saying, **". . . declare thou, that thou mayest be justified."**

Immediately, he said, "What I drank was water; any other thing can remain in the bottle."

Believe me, till this day, this young man is still very much alive. Glory to God!

It also makes God to fool your doctors and those who think you cannot do anything to change your situation, when your word is confirmed (Isaiah 44:24-26; Mark 5:21-24, 35-42; John 11:11-44).

3.	Acting on God's word: this is a booster to what you confessed.

*"What doth it profit, my brethren, though a man say he hath faith and have not works? Can faith save him"* (James 2:14)

*"For not the hearers of the law are just before God, but the doers of the word shall be justified"* (Romans 2:13)

*"But be ye doers of the word, and not hearers only, deceiving your own selves. But whoso looketh into the perfect law of liberty, and continueth therein, he being not a forgetful hearer, but a doer of the work, this man shall be blessed in his deed"* (James 1:22,25)

So with all these Scriptures, what are you presently doing to affect your vision? I mean, to bring your dream to reality. It is your actions that prove that you have believed what God said to you about your future that will make God crown your faith with enviable result(s).

In conclusion, the faith that works is not the one you conjured by putting yourself into metaphysical activity, but that which came alive in you, with its spirit that makes it compel you into positive confessions and actions, as the rhema of God—the living word. This is the faith that works or, you can call it, **"the workable faith."**

It will surely work for you in Jesus' name!

If God has not spoken to you concerning a purpose through divine revelation, this kind of workable faith for successful accomplishment will never come to your heart. It does not tally with personal ambition that is outside God's plan and purpose for your life. Therefore, I advise you to go for divine vision, and not ambition.

# FAITH BOOSTERS

A booster is something that makes one feel more confident according to the Oxford Advanced Learner's dictionary. It also defines the word "boost" as "to increase the strength or value of something." Therefore, faith boosters are spiritual devices or elements that increase or improve the strength and value of faith in order to maximize its usefulness and its output or delivery.

The following elements or factors boost your confidence in God concerning the pursuit of your purpose; they are the boosters of faith.

1.  Love for God and for mankind (Galatians. 5:6; Matthew 22:37, 40; 1 John 3:14; 2:9-11). Faith operates only in the environment of God's kind of life. This life contains the characteristics of God (Galatians 5:22 1 John 3: 17).
2.  Covenant mentality (Deuteronomy 7:7-15; Psalm 89:33, 34; Jeremiah 33:20, 21). God is the God of covenant. If you know that God does not break a covenant, you will always be confident in God's word and promises for your life.

*"Seek ye out of the book of the Lord, and read: no one of these shall fail, none shall want her mate: for my mouth it hath commanded, and his spirit hath gathered them"* (Isaiah 34:16).

Remember, God is faithful to his covenant promises; not even the devil can go beyond them to do anything against your purpose and destiny.

3.  The sense of spiritual political dominion by the understanding of spiritual hierarchy. That is, after God, man; after man, angels of God; after them, Satan and his cohort. Everything is under the dominion of Christ (Philippians 2:9-11), who now puts them under man (Psalm. 8:4-8; Psalm 82:6; Matthew 19:16; Luke 10:19; Isaiah 45:12; Genesis 1:26, 27; Romans 13:1-2; Ephesians 1:19-23). All these scriptures show us that heaven overseas the earth through man in the name of Jesus. Everything under the heavens is answerable to man, who in turn is answerable to Jesus, who is then answerable to God the Father. You are a god to Satan, his evil angels, sicknesses and diseases, sorrow, and all manner of evil works.

Purpose mentality: a man of purpose is like someone possessing a prominent position in a company. The company backs every official duty he embarks on with every needed necessity for a successful journey.

Now when you come to the acknowledgement of all those boosters, they will serve as catalysts that will quicken your steps of faith.

## THE BENEFITS OF A MAN ON PURPOSE

a.   Provision (Philippians 4:19; Psalm 33:18, 19). For example: finance, accommodation, mobility, constant angelic help or intervention, miscellaneous, etc.
b.   Protection (Zechariah 2:8; Psalm. 121:1-8)
c.   Long life (Exodus 23:26; Psalm 91:14-16)
d.   Good health (1 John 2; Exodus 23:25)
e.   Rewards (Mark 10:28-30)

They are known as divine providence.

## ENEMIES OF FAITH

Have you ever asked yourself why your faith is unproductive sometimes? Let me help you out by showing you the reasons behind the misery that could be surrounding your faith:

1.   Absence of divine love: the fuel that makes the engine of your faith to function (Galatians 5:6). If you don't show love to people, your faith will never work. Divine love attracts God's presence (Ephesians 3:16-19). God's presence gives no room for impossibility (Mark 10:27) and causes unusual breakthroughs (Psalm 114:1-8).
2.   Human traditions (Mark 3:1-6; 7:7, 9, 13): this talks about human laws that are contrary to the word of God.
3.   Negative scientific reports (1 Timothy 6:20): they seem to be real in the eyes of natural or carnal man. They are facts, but they can work contrary to faith. God's word is the truth, but facts of science can be used by the devil against the truth of God's word to demean or destroy faith. Satan works within the limit of science (Romans 4:17-21). To Abraham, science said that his manhood was dead, and that his wife, Sarah, had passed her menopause. To the woman

with the issue of blood, her case was closed by science; but faith delivered her out of her situation. Hallelujah! (1 Corinthians 1:20, 22-25).

4.  Human philosophy: this talk about the common beliefs of men based on their experiences and discoveries outside God's word, and they do not agree with God's word (Colossians 2:8). It can also be identified with a statement like **"There is the saying that"**, which may not be in agreement with God's covenant promises. Be careful of such!

5.  Unstable, wavering mind (James 1:5-8).

6.  Doubt (Mark 11:23; Hebrews 4: 1-3).

7.  Procrastination (Hebrews 11:1; Acts 14:8-10; Mark 3:1-6). All those scriptures convince us not to that there is no room for procrastination. Just have a 'do-it-now' mentality, when things are meant to be done immediately.

8.  Fear (Hebrews 2:15; Proverbs 29:25). Until you conquer fear and do what God says you should do, you may remain in bondage of staying in one position forever.

9.  Paying attention to mockery and destructive criticism. Please pay deaf ears to critics and mockers, except they are helping you to discover your mistakes that need to be corrected. There is no great man without a scar on his name.

10. Alternatives: putting your confidence in some other one or things order than God (Jeremiah 17:5-7; Psalm 121:1, 2; James 1:17; Psalm 123:1, 2; Palms 60:11, 12).

11. And lastly, staying in the atmosphere of negative confessions (Psalm 1:1-3; John 11:11-14; Mark 5:21-24, 35-42). This one is very dangerous, except that you can fight the good fight of faith by countering the words with God's word, when they come around you. But peradventure you cannot do so, shift your boat away from those kinds of environment.

## THE TRIAL OF FAITH

I have discovered by virtue of study that the beginning of everything is always hard. Once a vision is born in a man, everything around him will wake up, including the devil and life itself.

*"For a great door and effectual is opened unto me, and there are many adversaries"* (1 Corinthians 16:9)

*"But he that received the seed into stony place, the same is he that heareth the word, and anon with joy receiveth it; yet hath he not root in himself, but dureth for a while: for when tribulation or persecution ariseth because of the word, by and by he is offended"* (Matthew13: 20,21)

When the word of the Lord comes to you, it brings to you a life of direction, for such word from the Lord births a vision to live for. This is when he tells you what to do in life with regards to purpose. As soon as this word comes, hardship, troubles, oppositions, tribulations, etc. will definitely arise against you in order to frustrate you from going ahead with your vision. But, just remember, all these things are just to try your faith in the Lord (1Peter 1:6, 7, 9).

## The University Of Tears

*"Wherein ye greatly rejoice, though now for a season, if need be, ye are in heaviness through manifold temptations: that the trial of your faith, being much more precious than of gold that perisheth, though it be tried with fire, might be found unto praise and honour and glory at the appearing of Jesus Christ"* (1 Peter 1:6-7)

I don't know what God has told you regarding his promises. I don't know what vision you are running with for the Lord now, and I don't know what you are presently passing through. I want to tell you that the end of your affliction is at hand.

God normally shows people what they should do in life, and also shows them how it will look like, but he will not show them the gap between the beginning of prophecy and the end of prophecy. Or sometimes, he will show you, depending on your spiritual maturity.

For example, he revealed the nature of Jesus' purpose from the beginning to the end. But in the case of the Israelites, he only told Abraham what they would experience with Pharaoh and what they would enjoy in Canaan, and he did not tell them what they would pass through on their way to Canaan.

Let me tell you how they experienced their pains:

*"And thou shalt remember all the way which the Lord thy God led thee these forty years in the wildness, to humble thee, and to prove thee, to know what was in thine heart, whether thou wouldest keep his commandments, or no. And he humbled thee and suffered thee to hunger and fed thee with manna, which thou knewest not, neither did thy fathers know; that he might make thee know that man doth not live by bread only, but by every word that proceedeth out of the mouth of the Lord doth man live. Thy raiment was not old upon thee; neither did thy foot swell, these forty years. Thou shalt also consider in thine heart that, as a man chasteneth his son, so the Lord thy God chasteneth thee"* (Deuteronomy 8:2-5)

This is really a University of Tears. There are different courses in this university:

a.   Humility

b.   Proof of a man's heart, if he can keep God's commandment, as he instructs him daily via rhema or logos

In the case of Jesus, the Holy Spirit drove him into a wilderness experience of hunger and thirst for forty days to be tempted of the devil (Matt. 4:1-11). As there was hunger, the tempter came. God wanted to test him and see if he would keep his commandments; and he passed the test of God (the trial of faith) successfully.

You can't carry God's mission without him proving your faithfulness. What about the case of Adam? God gave him the assignment of dressing the Garden of Eden (Genesis 2:15). And according to the usual manner of God, he allowed the devil to test him and see if he would keep his word, but Adam failed. May you not fail in Jesus' name!

God must always prove people's heart to know if they will really follow him. He does not believe in sentiment or assumption.

c.   The next course in this university is discovery. Making you know that Kingdom life is not meat and bread nor a bed of roses, but that you must learn to know that the just shall live by faith—the substance that proceeds out of God's word.

*"For therein is the righteousness of God revealed from faith to faith: as it is written, the just shall live by faith"* (Romans 1:17)

d.  The next course in this university is the course where God shows you his sustaining power.

*"Thy raiment waxed not old upon thee, neither did thy foot swell, these forty years"* (Deuteronomy 8:4)

e.  The next course also is 'Provisionology' (the study of God's power of providence).

*"And he humbled thee, and suffered thee to hunger, and fed thee with manna . . ."* (Deuteronomy 8:3a)

He is Jehovah Jireh.

Look at how David, the Psalmist, graded the courses in this university of tears: *"For thou, O God, hast proved us: thou hast tried us as silver is tried. Thou broughtest us into the net; thou laidst affliction upon our loins. Thou hast caused men to ride over our heads; we went through fire and through water: but thou broughtest us out into a wealthy place"* (Psalm 66:10-12).

A wealthy place in life is God's reward or divine certificate. That is, at this point, God will now employ you into his field and appoint you your lot because he can now trust you. And then his favor will begin to flow towards you from measure to measure, according to the demand of your vision or purpose from time to time; and from phase to phase, as you grow in your pursuit of purpose.

God's favor is his provision for the accomplishment of his assignment by segments.

*"But my God shall supply all your needs according to his riches in glory by Christ Jesus"* (Philippians 4:19)

As I earlier said in this book, though he gave you a big assignment, there are smaller assignments ranging from its beginning to the end. And that is why a great success is the result of the accumulation or summation of smaller successes.

God's favor is his provision for your enjoyment.

*"Charge them that are rich in this world, that they be not high-minded, nor trust in uncertain riches, but in the living God, who giveth us richly all things to enjoy"* (1 Timothy 6:17)

You can clearly see that God is not a waster. Whatever God brought your way has a reason for it. Even Jesus commanded that the fragments from the miracle of fish and bread multiplication should be gathered.

*"When they were filled, he said unto his disciples, Gather up the fragments that remain, that nothing be lost"* (John 6:12)

God's favor also provides you with seeds for the expansion of His Kingdom.

*"Now he that ministereth seed to the sower . . ."* (2 Corinthians 9:10)

God's favor is the extension of God's hand for your good. When God passes you out of the University of Tears, he brings you out of your desert and howling wilderness, and takes you to the high places of the earth—the wealthy place.

*"For the Lord's portion is his people; Jacob is the lot of his inheritance. He found him in a desert land and in the waste-howling wilderness (Egypt, a place of affliction); he led him about, he instructed him, he kept him as the apple of his eye . . . He made him ride on the high places of the earth . . ."* (Deuteronomy 32:9, 10, 13, Paraphrased)

The high places of the earth are where good things can begin to happen unconditionally to your favor. In this place, there is no struggle, but the determined people get there. Everything is easy there. You will get there in Jesus' mighty name!

Don't forget about the man Joseph. God showed him the throne, but he never showed him what would happen on his way to the throne. Although he passed through harsh situations, he never stopped moving forward with his life. So whatever that is happening to you now is neither your rest nor your end yet; just keep moving because, no matter what happens, you cannot change the program of divinity meant for you.

Hear what one of the graduates of the University of Tears, even the man Job, said:

*"But he knoweth the way that I take: when he hath tried me, I shall come forth as gold. My foot hath held his steps, his way have I kept, and not declined. Neither have I gone back from the commandment of his lips; I have esteemed the words of his mouth more than my necessary food. But he is in one mind, and who can turn him? And what his soul desireth, even that he doeth. For he performeth the thing that is appointed for me: and many such things are with him"* (Job 23:10-14)

Jeremiah also said, *"O Lord, I know that the way of man is not in himself: it is not in man that walketh to direct his steps"* (Jeremiah 10:23).

This is to show you that you cannot dictate how your life should go because; your ways are not in your hands but in the hand of God.

The bible says, *"Man's goings are of the Lord; how can a man then understand his own way?"* (Proverbs 20:24).

So it is God's undeniable mandate to take you through the University of Tears, and he chooses your course for you there.

*"I the Lord search the heart, I try the reins, even to give every man according to his ways, and according to the fruit of his doings"* (Jeremiah 17:10)

So don't strive against the season of divine trials. That is why you should have the understanding of times and seasons, so that you would not waste your time and energy in swimming against the ocean of your destiny.

*"Woe to him that striveth with his maker . . ."* (Isaiah 45:9a)

All you need to do is to fulfill the following scripture during such seasons: *"In every thing give thanks: for this is the will of God in Christ Jesus concerning you"* (1 Thessalonians 5:17).

Because after your travail, I am sure you will definitely bring forth your male child just like the people of Zion.

*"Who hath heard such a thing? Who hath seen such a thing? Shall the earth be made to bring forth in one day? Or shall a nation be born at once? For as soon as Zion travailed, she brought forth her children"* (Isaiah 66:8)

Trust in God; for God cannot put a vision on your inside without helping you to put it to birth. You are the only one that can stop Him.

*"Shall I bring to the birth, and not cause to bring forth? saith the Lord"* (Isaiah 66:9)

So, no matter the pain, don't worry; your day of deliverance shall soon arrive, if you don't give up. The Lord is on your side!

## Delay is not denial

Your victory in life over your circumstances depends on the strength of your faith.

*"For whatsoever is born of God overcometh the world: and this is the victory that overcometh the world, even our faith"* (1 John 5:4)

*"If thou faint in the day of adversity, thy strength is small"* (Proverbs 24:10)

So work on your faith to make it grow; and guide it properly, considering the fact that the devil's business is to make sure your faith in God, concerning your pursuit, dies.

Jesus said to Peter,

*". . . Simon, Simon, behold, Satan hath desired to have you, that he may sift you as wheat; but I have prayed for thee, that thy 'faith' fail not . . ."* (Luke 22:32,33a)

It is real that sometimes, it seems as if God had left you or has forgotten you. Never listen to your feelings or to your situations. Remember what I told you (in chapter four) that if you give the devil attention, he will give you direction; and if you obey him, he will sift you out of the way to your fulfillment. Just believe that God is with you, and that he is in the business of making you for your own glory.

God says, *"When thou passest through the waters, I will be with thee; and through the rivers, they shalt not overflow thee: when thou walkest through the fire, thou shalt not be burned; neither shall the flame kindle upon thee"* (Isaiah 43:2).

In all that the Israelites went through, the following promise was a shield about them:

*"In all their affliction he was afflicted, and the angel of his presence saved them: in his love and in his pity he redeemed them; and bare them, and carried them all the days of old"* (Isaiah 63:9)

If God helped them out because of his covenant with them, he will surely respect his covenant with you also.

*"For we have not an high priest which cannot be touched with the feelings of our infirmities . . ."* (Hebrews 4: 15)

Now God is asking you, saying, *"Can a woman forget her suckling child, that she should not have compassion on the son of her womb? Yea, they may forget, yet will I not forget thee"* (Isaiah 49:15).

So, wait on the Lord!

Look at what the psalmist said: *"I waited patiently for the Lord; and he inclined unto me, and heard my cry. He brought me up also out of an horrible pit, out of the miry clay, and set my feet upon a rock and established my goings"* (Psalm 40; 1-2).

And he continued, saying, *"And he put a new song in my mouth, even praise unto our God; many shall see it and fear, and shall trust in the lord"* (Psalm 40: 3).

I wish you were in King David's time to see what the pursuit of Saul against him caused him. It was a rigor. But see what he said, *"When the Lord turned again the captivity of Zion, we were like them that dream. Then was our mouth filled with laughter, and our tongue with singing: then said they among the heathen, the Lord hath done great things for them"* (Psalm 126: 1-2).

When your turn comes, your captivity will beg for your leave, as Egypt begged the children of Israel to leave their country. So, never give up your faith concerning your future!

*"For to him that is joined to the living there is hope: for a living dog is better than a dead lion"* (Ecclesiastes 9: 4)

Remember what the Almighty God said, *"For I know the thoughts that I think toward you saith the lord, thoughts of good not of evil, to give you an expected end"* (Jeremiah 29: 11).

You will get there in Jesus' name!

## TRIALS AND TEMPTATIONS

How do you view trials and temptation? I see them as examinations of life we must pass, or else we remain backward. Before every glory, there is fire; before every crown, there is a cross; before every top, there is a pit; before every appearance of light, there is darkness.

Sometimes the trial of your moral may come. Remember Joseph and Potiphar's wife. Sometimes material temptation may come. Remember Achan. There are many dangerous women who are looking for young and matured men of precious life and future that they can pull out of the way.

*"Lust not after her beauty in thine heart; neither let her take thee with her eyelids. For by means of a whorish woman, a man is brought to a piece of bread: and an adulteress will hunt for the precious life"* (Proverbs 6: 25, 26)

They don't look for just any man. When they see a man that is going somewhere in life, they know. So, be careful! Remember, it is your proving time. Hardship is not a criterion or excuse for you to fall into wrong hands. Many who have fallen into pits are crying for a divine help today. So, don't make such a silly mistake. I pray God will deliver such people out of such pits, and that God will guide you out of the paths of such pits with his good eyes also. You will make it to your future!

I want you to see those temptation and trial times as passages to your great future, because, *"As the fining pot for silver and the furnace for gold; so is a man to his praise" (Proverbs 27:21).*

See what Apostle Peter said, *"But the God of all grace, who has called us unto his eternal glory by Christ Jesus, after that you have suffered a while, restore, establish, strengthen, settle you"* (1 Peter 5:10).

Jesus also said that there is only one narrow road to great tomorrow; only few people are already on it. So you have to be violent to enter into it.

*"Enter ye in at the strait gate: for wide is the gate, and broad is the way, that leadeth unto destruction, and many there be which go in thereat: because strait is the gate, and narrow is the way, which leadeth unto life, and few there be that find it"* (Matthew 7: 13, 14)

*"The law and the prophets were until John: since that time the kingdom of God is preached, and every man presseth into it"* (Luke 16: 16)

Therefore, you must press yourself into your future of good life. The Lord is on your side!

**How to overcome your trials**

Be willing to pass your exams. Before every promotion to a new level in life, there must be exams of life. Mind you, the exams that God will allow you to pass through are not above you.

*"There hath no temptation taken you but such as is common to man: but God is faithful, who will not suffer you to be tempted above that ye are able. But will with the temptation also make a way to escape, that you may be able to bear it"* (1 Corinthians 10: 13)

So if you fail, never blame God or anyone. Count it as your fault. God will keep you from falling in Jesus' name!

*"Who are kept by the power of God through faith unto salvation, ready to be revealed in the last time"* (1 Peter 1: 5)

*"Now unto him that is able to keep you from falling . . "* (Jude 24)

Have a vision of an enviable tomorrow through God's Word. Just as in the case of Jesus.

*". . . Who for the joy that was set before him endured the cross, despising the shame . . ."* (Hebrews 12: 2)

If you don't have a mental picture of your tomorrow, you are bound to break out on the way because of what you may be passing through.

Keep rejoicing. Remember, the absence of joy may destroy your vision of God's plan for you. So don't let your joy die (Joel 1:12). Always give God thanks (Habakkuk 3: 7-19). Also, remember that the Lord is doing everything for your own good (Romans 8: 28).

Eat enough of God's word; the journey is long (Colossians 3:16). Remember, it is food that gives strength for a living.

*"He giveth power to the faint; and to them that have no might he increaseth strength. Even the youths shall faint and be weary, and the young men shall utterly fall, but they that wait upon the Lord shall renew their strength; they shall mount up with wings as eagles; they shall run, and not be weary, they shall walk and not faint"* (Isaiah 40: 29-31)

Many have made shipwreck of their faith by thinking that waiting upon the Lord means keeping their hands in their bosom and just gazing at heaven for a down-pour. Waiting really means to tarry in anticipation of something. But while tarrying, there is every need for you to keep praying and studying the word of God, feeding your soul with the engrafted word of faith.

*"Wherefore lay apart all filthiness and superfluity of naughtiness, and receive with meekness the engrafted word, which is able to save your souls"* (James 1:21)

*"Through desire a man, having separated himself, seeketh and intermeddleth with all wisdom"* (Proverbs 18:1)

This is what you should be doing to keep you going forward. You have to give yourself continually to God's word (wisdom) to enable you, receive strength day by day because,

*"A wise man is strong; yea a man of knowledge increaseth strength. If thou faint in the day of adversity, thy strength is small"* (Proverbs 24:5, 10)

*"Wisdom strengtheneth the wise more than ten mighty men which are in the city"* (Ecclesiastes 7:19)

*"Get wisdom, get understanding: forget it not; neither decline from the words of my mouth. Forsake her not, and she shall preserve thee: love her, and she shall keep thee"* (Proverbs 4:5-6)

*"This book of the law shall not depart out of thine mouth; but thou shalt meditate therein day and night, that thou mayest observe to do according to all that is written therein: for then thou shalt make your way prosperous, and thou shalt have good success"* (Joshua 1:8)

## Satanic winds for faith trial

When passing through your trial times, the following are what the devil uses to frustrate your vision:

1.  Mockery
2.  Shame: he makes sure you get ashamed by moving people to mock at you, especially when result has not begun to roll in.
3.  Contempt: he will make people ignore you and your vision. Sometimes, when your vision has not started manifesting fully, nobody will like to identify with you. So the devil uses this medium to attack your faith daily, just to make sure your faith concerning your vision dies down.
4.  Fear of persons and death: he also threatens you with statements like "your father should not hear this," or "none of those people who trod this same track ever lived long." But I encourage you to strengthen yourself in the word of God, and never give up.
5.  Criticisms: remember that most critics are those who have no focus in life or those that are afraid of your success.

All these are the winds the devil will surely organize against you on your way to fulfilling your destiny. Ask every great man who ever made it; they will tell you their own side of the story. There is no great man without a negative history. So never fear anything.

You may ask if they also experienced fear at all. Yes, they surely did, but they summoned courage. A wise man said, "Courage is not the absence of fear, but it is going against the voice of fear for conquest."

**How can we overcome these winds?**

1. Be willing to carry your Cross (1 Peter 2:12-15; 2 Corinthians 4:8-9; 16-18).
2. Let the love and compassion of the people, whose solution you are carrying, possess your soul; and let the fear of God who sent you fill your heart, because if you don't fulfill your vision, you will give account of everything when you get to heaven.
3. Never be afraid when you pass through the shadow of death, for God is with you. Bishop David O. Oyedepo, the presiding Bishop of Living Faith Church (Nigeria) and some other great men have their stories to tell you, if you care to find out.
4. Stand upon the word of God! Make God's word your foundation and let it be the base of your action or every step you take in your life (Matthew 7:24-27).
5. Have patience and be willing to suffer long, in case it spells to be so. Sometimes, the devil will show you a ten-mile suffering. Tell him your strength can carry you through a hundred miles, and then you will see him get tired of you, and bow away from your sight. It is only when the devil sees that you fear suffering always and do look for comfort that he threatens you with the heat thereof. But see this,

*"That ye be not slothful, but followers of them who through faith and patience inherit the promise"* (Hebrews 6:12)

By this way also, you will make it. Read what Jesus said in Revelation 3:10.

**7 keys for persistence**

*"The law and the prophets were until John: since that time the kingdom of God is preached, and every man presseth into it"* (Luke 16:16)

In the Kingdom of God, only persistent people get the crown of life. To persist means to continue to do something with determination in spite of difficulties, opposition and failure, and refusing to give up.

*"Know ye not that they which run in a race run all, but one receiveth the price? So run, that ye may obtain"* (1 Corinthians 9:24)

Jesus said, *"For which of you, intending to build a tower, sitteth not down first, and counteth the cost, whether he has sufficient to finish it? Lest haply, after he hath laid the foundation, and is not able to finish it, all that behold it begin to mock him, saying, this man began to build, and was not able to finish"* (Luke 14:28-30)

This is talking about a man who fails because he does not plan his work well. But what if you have planned well and cannot continue? You will be mocked also because eyes are watching you.

Jesus said, *". . . No man, having put his hand to the plow, and looking back is fit for the kingdom of God"* (Luke 9:62).

In case you think of drawing back, remember that Israel had the same mind, but God was not happy with them.

See what God said, *"Now the just shall live by faith; but if any man draw back, my soul shall have no pleasure in him"* (Hebrews 10:38).

You can now see that there is no hope for those who draw back.

*"But we are not of them who draw back unto perdition; but of them that believe to the saving of our soul"* (Hebrews 10:39)

Praise God! Hallelujah! May God be your strength in Jesus' name!

But if we must persist for us to make it and be rewarded for our pursuit, what then are the keys for persistence?

1.  Have a true vision of divine purpose. That is, make sure you are pursuing a divine assignment. God will never comfort you for what he never sent you, for everyone of man's plan will fail unless it matches with God's plan for him. So find out God's plan for your life and pursue same.

*"Many plans are in a man's mind, but it is the Lord's purpose for him that will stand" (Proverbs 19:21, AMP)*

So never pursue your personal ambition, for it is subject to failure.

2.   Have proper information (light) from heaven or clearance from God himself about your purpose and be sure of it very well.
3.   Have a result consciousness. Know that God hates unfruitfulness (Isaiah 5:1-15; Luke 13:6-9; Mark 11:12-14, 20, 21).
4.   Be willing to succeed. Let your name be counted among the great and successful people, and let it be recorded in the Guinness Book of Records.
5.   Have faith that God will surely bring it to pass (Ezekiel 12:22-25; Romans 8:17-21).
6.   Increase your passion for your vision by listening to and reading about other people's successes and testimonies.
7.   Apply the law of self-suggestion or autosuggestion. That is, keep reminding yourself the knowledge of the revelation God gave to you and the vision of the benefits or results God showed to you. If possible, I suggest you write it somewhere you can easily see it (Habakkuk 2:2). The Lord is on your side! You will make it in Jesus' name!

## REWARDS FOR OVERCOMING

The crown of life is only meant for the victors of life's challenges (James 1:12). God does not reward excuses for defeat. He only rewards victory. He does not reckon with failures but with those who triumphed over their circumstances in life. So you have no reason to fail.

I have heard of a man who has no legs, but is a Pastor with a wife and children. He has also with him five associate Pastors in Ghana. I don't know what may be your disadvantage now, but I am sure that if you can think very well, you may discover that it is your asset for great success in life. May God open your eyes!

Greatness in life is a product that begins its journey in the mind. So, if you can make proper use of your mind, you will go places. Therefore, make no room for excuses.

The rewards for overcoming are: a. the high places of the earth— prominence and fame (Deuteronomy 32:10,13) b. a wealthy place (Psalm 66:12) c. the crown of life (James 1:12) d. Possession of your soul; no hypertension (Luke 21:19) e. Promotion into a manifestation season (Luke 1:80) f. a place of rest on every side, etc.

These shall be your portions in Jesus' name!

*"Cast not away therefore your confidence, which hath great recompense of reward. For ye have need of patience, that, after ye have done the will of God ye might receive the promise"* (Hebrews 10:35, 36)

*". . . For the vision is yet for an appointed time, but at the end it shall speak, and not lie . . ."* (Habakkuk 2:2a)

Hello! I see your reward coming. But when it comes, remember me in your Kingdom! God bless you! (Laugh)!

# CHAPTER NINE

## ARISE AND SHINE: GET OUT OF THE NEST

*"What doth it profit, my brethren, though a man say he hath faith, and have no works? Can faith save him? For as the body without the spirit is dead, so faith without works is dead also"* (James 2:14, 26)

*"Prepare thy work without, and make it fit for thyself in the field; and afterwards build thine house"* (Proverbs 24:27)

Hallelujah! If you've got the right vision of your divine purpose from Jehovah, the revealer of secrets; you've believed it with all your heart, nothing wavering; you've undergone both divine and natural training well enough for a start, and you, sure, have acquired enough stamina to begin your journey, and you are on time and in the right divine geographical location, by spiritual sensitivity; it is therefore, your time to arise and get out of your incubating nest, and begin the journey God has placed before you. Begin now to put your faith into action in order to fulfill your destiny.

God said to Jeremiah the prophet, *"Thou therefore, gird up thy loins, and arise, and speak unto them all that I command thee . . ."* (Jeremiah 1:17)**.**

God showed him his purpose in verse five, then in this verse seventeen, he asked him to prepare for his ministry **(gird up your loins),** and then he said, **"begin to speak the things I command thee"** God believes in preparation, but he hates slothfulness.

The bible says, *"The slothful man roasteth not that which he took in hunting: but the substance of a diligent man is precious"* (Proverbs 12:27).

So it is time you roasted that meat (idea) you got from hunting (the realm of revelation). Any further delay may damn your vision and render it unproductive completely; and except God help you, you may never make it up again.

*"By much slothfulness the building decayeth: and through idleness of the hands the house droppeth through"* (Ecclesiastes 10:18)

Please don't let your zeal die by being slothful. Rise up to your responsibility! Fulfill your destiny!

## FULFILLING YOUR DESTINY

Destiny cannot be fulfilled by merely talking about it. Again, never keep planning till you go out of time.

What makes people delay the pursuit of their purpose discovered is mostly waiting for a more convenient time and a bulky financial capital. God has not given man any extra time for wastage. I have told you before that God may not allow you to start big.

In order to fulfill your destiny, the following are unavoidable:

a.   Have a pursuit mentality.

*"In all labour there is profit: but the talk of the lips tendeth only to penury"* (Proverbs 14:23)

Behind every working machine, there is manpower. Nothing works on its own.

Now you may say, "What about electrical appliances?" I tell you, if there is no human operational effect on them, they will never work. So don' wait unnecessarily and waste your life; do something about your vision. Jesus said, *"I must work the works of him that sent me, while it is day: the night cometh, when no man can work"* (John 9:4).

That was completely a work mentality! So, be a real follower of Jesus, if you really want to fulfill your destiny.

b.  Avoid procrastination. *"Say not ye, There are yet four months, and then cometh harvest? Behold, I say unto you, Lift up your eyes, and look on the fields; for they are white already to harvest!" (John 4:35).*

The more you procrastinate your pursuit, the more your ripe fruits will drop and get rot. So, be on time. Make hay while sun shine!

c.  Put your hands on the desk by determination (Luke 9:62; 2Kings 7:3-9), avoiding unnecessary excuses (Proverbs 22:13; Psalm 121:7; 8; Proverbs 21:31), avoiding time wasters (Proverbs 28:19), and program your days with reasonable schedule. Fill your time with necessary priorities; make good use of your time. Don't allow visitors at your work place or during work time.

d.  Make good priority on your income based on the order of necessity, and be sure you have savings for the future.

## THE PURSUIT OF PURPOSE

*"Know ye not that they which run in a race run all, but one receiveth the price? So, run, that ye may obtain."* (1 Corinthians 9:24)

God never rewards you for receiving the vision of your purpose, but he rewards the daily achievement of your purpose from phase to phase.

There are two mediums through which man can access the rewards of God on earth and in heaven:

1.  The labor of our hands (Deuteronomy 28:12)
2.  The liberality of our soul and generosity of our hands (Deuteronomy 12:6-7; Isaiah 58:10-12; Proverbs 11:24, 25)

Let us discuss the labor of our hands. God believes and takes pleasure in those who carry out divine plan. It doesn't matter how you begin your journey, provided you are within the divine program for your purpose. No destiny begins big. Every great destiny today started small. A journey of one mile begins with a step. Little drops of water make a mighty ocean. So despise not the days of little beginnings.

*"Though thy beginning was small, yet thy latter end should greatly increase"* (Job 8:7).

## THE FORCE OF WORK

Work is the means through which mental pictures or visions come to reality. It is the means through which our dreams in life are being transmuted into their physical equivalence. Nobody really knows the dream that you are pregnant with until you travail in labor to bring it forth before the eyes of people.

## WHAT IS WORK

Let us look at the following dictionary definition of work:

It is the use of physical strength or mental power in order to do or make something.

It is the use of force to produce movement.

The word "work" connotes activity towards making profits; but working for salary only just to earn a living is never a 'Purpose'. Many people are just going around with different activities, but they are going nowhere in life. Ambition is never progressive but circulatory, while vision or divine purpose (because God is involved, who gives instruction from time to time to bring about sequential progress) is progressive in nature. Ambition does not have an end in view, but vision does because God reveals the end of it to the bearer. If you are pursuing any goal that you don't really know how the end will look like, please drop it. Don't waste your time, energy and money for what does not concern your destiny.

It is true that the beginning of everything is hard, but you need to be courageous enough for a take-off. Have this in mind: to begin an assignment is halfway the journey. Work should arise out of your mind to affect your generation and the world around you.

Vision will show you pictures of what can be or will come to pass, but a vision not translated into a mission (work) is a daydream. God demands that every vision given you should be worked out. Our covenant fathers that ever had their destinies fulfilled were men that worked.

* Abraham was a worker (Genesis 13:2)

* Isaac was a worker (Genesis 26:1-14)

* Jacob was a worker. He served Laban for twenty years (Genesis 31:41)

* Joseph was a worker (Genesis 39:3-6; 21-23)

* Daniel was a worker (Daniel 6:1-3)

* Nehemiah was a worker (Nehemiah 1-2:12-18)

* Ezra was a worker (Ezra 7)

* Jesus was also a worker (John 5:17)

In the case of Jesus, when someone threatened him, mentioning King Herod, he refused to depart from his work.

*"The same day there came certain of the Pharisees, saying unto him, Get thee out, and depart hence: for Herod will kill thee and he said unto them, Go ye, and tell that fox, Behold, I cast out devils, and I do cures today and tomorrow, and the third day I shall be perfected"* (Luke 13:31,23)

Nothing makes purpose glorious like work. So, pray as if everything depends on God, but work as if everything depends on you.

## WHY MUST YOU WORK OUT YOUR DREAM?

1. It gives meaning to your faith; that is, what you believe and confess (James 2:14).
2. It provides you an opportunity to accomplish your dream.
3. It is profiting (Proverbs 14:23). The difference between a poor man and the rich is that, while the poor man's strength and ability will lie inside him, the rich man works to release what is on the inside of him. Your potential is like a raw material that contains

your wealth; until you process and sell it, there will be no gain. The taste of the pudding is in the eating.

4.  It establishes your honor and dignity in life.
5.  It helps you to reveal who you really are.
6.  It enhances your self-esteem.
7.  It gives you the opportunity to enjoy success.
8.  It makes you a blessing to others (Ephesians 4:28)

## THE NECESSARY INGREDIENTS FOR THE SUCCESSFUL PURSUIT OF PURPOSE

In the course of your journey, there are certain things you must do to enhance your pursuit and make it possible.

1.  Obey the 'law of devotion'. Mount an altar of prayer where you and God will always meet: a. to take instructions for daily goings. b. for God to make you aware of the enemy's plans against your vision c. to be corrected for any error made in the past that you might not even be aware of. d. to be aware of the next move of God. e. to allow divine insight in order to know how to go about the work, etc. (After finishing your present phase, always ask God to show you where to go from where you are).
2.  Be an information seeker. Be a researcher.
3.  Seek divine wisdom in everything you do (James 1:5).
4.  What you know you can do today; don't postpone.
5.  Don't fail to plan before carrying out your ideas (Proverbs. 24:27; Luke 14:28-32)
6.  Follow the leadings of the Holy Spirit in your life. Your success lies in Him. So be sensitive to Him.
7.  Maintain good health physically, mentally and spiritually. Learn to seek the counsel of a godly medical adviser, whenever you feel physiologically funny.
8.  Watch against money and sexual temptations. They are dangerous to spiritual health. Remember, it is your spirit that is linked with God. If it is damned, you are gone, except by the grace of God; and even if you are restored, it will still take you time to be restored in your soul. So beware!
9.  Be persistent. If really you are seeing a great tomorrow, then you need to press forward (see seven keys for persistence in chapter

eight). A successful life is all about progress. Someone said, "If you stand too long in a place, they will mistake you for a statue." So never fear the oppositions of life and thereby be bound on a spot for too long.

## HOW TO CONTEND WITH THE CHALLENGES OF LIFE

When God spoke to Moses to move Israel from Egypt to Canaan, he did not say, "Well, if I see a Red Sea on the way, I will know that God didn't speak to me." When God gives you the land of Canaan, don't think that it is free of the Anakin (Deuteronomy 1:28). In fact, they have been there before you began your journey. But I know that the God, who helped Israel in their time, will also help you in Jesus' name!

The broad way of life is full of fearful, indecisive failures, while the narrow-the way to success—is full of courageous winners of this life (Matthew 7:13, 14).

If you are looking for comfort in life on your way to Canaan, you may find little or none, and if you don't take care, you may never enter your Canaan. So be careful you don't drop your carcass in the wilderness of life as some Israelites did.

Listen, I have heard many winners make statement like "I have made it, but it was not easy. It took God's help."

From the first day you take your step to move from where you are not meant to be (Egypt, a place of bondage) to a place where your life will be fulfilled; or from what you are not meant for to what you are meant for, oppositions will want to stop you (1 Corinthians 16:9). So don't allow your dream to remain a dream till you die.

In fact, anyone who will want to stop you from possessing your Canaan (a place or thing you are really sure God is the one who showed it to you) wants you to really remain in slavery to a perpetual bondage.

When God has asked you to marry someone or to leave a particular job or town and go for another for the betterment of your life, don't always expect the road to be smooth. And that the road is not smooth at certain times should not make you doubt the voice of God that you heard, or the revelation he gave you.

Let's look at the ways to contend with the challenges of life:

1.  See them defeated already (Deuteronomy 2:24; Joshua 8:1, 2). Every time Israel wanted to fight with their enemies, God would always tell them he had already given them (enemies) into their (Israelites) hands. So see your enemies also in your hand already. If you can see yourself as a great person through divine revelation, then, nothing would be strong enough to stop your journey to your destination in life.
2.  See them as examinations you must pass to ensure your lifting (2 Peter 5:10; 2 Corinthians 4:4; 1 Peter 1:6-9).
3.  Always remember that challenges reveal your unknown, untapped, and undeveloped hidden abilities for a super success. Remember Gideon (Judges 6:12-14)!
4.  Know that challenges quicken your mind for excellent and productive thinking (Ecclesiastes 7:3).
5.  Know for sure that even if you fall on the sword, you will never be hurt (Joel 2:7, 8). Troubles or challenges on your way to your fulfillment are not designed to kill you but are for your promotion and are to make you shine as a star whenever you defeat them. So determine to win always.
6.  Know that you are born to overcome (1John 5:4).
7.  Make God your backbone (Psalm 146:3, 4; Romans 8:31; Psalm 22:45; 20:7-8).
8.  Learn to enquire from God on what to do to ensure your victory; take example from Moses (before the Red Sea and before the water of Marah) and King David (1 Samuel 23:1-5; 2 Samuel 5:17-25).
9.  Move forward and do what God wants you to do. Until you move forward, God will never act (Exodus 14:15-18, 21, 22).
10. Learn to challenge the mountains; do not fear them (Micah 6:1). Speak against your oppositions. Use your shield of faith (Ephesians 6:10-18; Job 6:25; Mark 11:23; 9:23; Hebrews 11:30, 32, 33).

After each victory, give God quality appreciation. Celebrate it by testifying (Psalm 64:9; 71:22-24).

# ENEMIES OF SUCCESS

So many people do not understand what the word 'Enemy' really is. But let me say this to you according to my view of what 'Enemy' really is: anything that will make you forget or put your vision aside is your enemy. An enemy is also whatever that distracts you from your vision or causes you to stumble with your vision or lose courage for its pursuit, or even causes you to lose your God-given helpers. Then, what are these things like?

1. Greed for money or materialism (Proverbs 15:27; 28:16, 20, 22; Timothy 6:6-10)
2. Lust over the opposite sex that is not your marital partner (1 Peter 2:11; Proverbs 2:16-19; 6:25-26, 27-32; 9:13-18)
3. Sin and fear (Numbers 14:6-9; Hebrews 2:15; Proverbs 29:25; 22:13; Jeremiah 5:25; Numbers 14:28-32)

## The fears that can possibly hinder you from fulfilling your purpose

1. Fear of criticism
2. Fear of mistake
3. Fear of mockery
4. Fear of rejection
5. Fear of failure
6. Fear of people

## How to cure these fears

1. Believe in your product (what you can offer to humanity). Believe in yourself.
2. Have this at the back of your mind: not everybody needs you in life. You are born to affect certain people and not everybody. E.g. doctors for the sick, bankers for financial issues, etc. So, give attention to those you are assigned to in life.
3. If rejection persists, rebuke the spirit behind it, except God did not send you to do what you are presently doing (James 4:7). Some of the things that can cause rejection are: a. being ahead of God b. not being in your divine place of assignment, c. not following divine instructions.

4.  For criticism, know this: if people misunderstand you, they will also misinterpret you. So this shouldn't move you at all. With time, you will be celebrated among them (Isaiah 60:14, 15, 16).

5.  Understand that most criticisms are mostly from those who are confused or wounded in life because of ignorance to where their lives should have followed. They lack direction and purpose for living; so, they spend their time chasing after the downfall of others.

Why? a. They fear your success because it exposes their nonentity. b. They do not understand the secret behind your success. c. They hate you because they just cannot be your rivals in your area of pursuit. This is why they spend their time organizing forces like slander, flattery and criticism against the work of your hand. Remember you can only overcome these people by paying them deaf ears, and pretend as if you have never heard their criticisms.

6.  Understand that mockery is a proof that the mocker hates your success. Sometimes, it can come to you because you failed in your target(s) due to lack of adherence to profitable guidance or counsel(s). But, remember, your failure never defines who you really are; you are only a success who has not known the right button(s) to press in order to ensure success or arrive in the place of your expectation. Just keep trying; never give up; you will surely get it right soon!

Remember Thomas Edison, who failed many times while trying to discover how electricity can work. When asked about his failure, he said he never failed, but discovered the many ways electricity cannot work. So, also, you should persist and break through with your pursuit.

7.  Understand you are not a perfect being. You are bound to make mistakes in life, but don't expect it at all. Nevertheless, if mistake happens, keep trying.

Anytime I make a mistake, I just quickly and humorously join my mockers to laugh at my foolishness and keep on going. Do the same and you will never feel anyone's mockery!

Never fear to take risks in life, because life is all about risks. A child who fears to take a step will never know how to run (Ecclesiastes 7:20).

8.  Understand that the person you fear will eventually master you.

9.  Don't welcome those who at all times despise your personal opinions or idea(s); or those who do not value you (who never count on you and who make you feel inferior before them). In fact, shift your boat away from them. Don't visit places, where you are despised. Don't live in such environment. Your destiny will be muted if you do. But your value, potentials, and abilities will be fully unlocked, appreciated, celebrated, awesomely welcomed and rewarded in places where you are respected. So go to those places; they are your divine geographical areas.

**Note:**

One of the greatest mistakes you will ever make is to think that you will do better in a place where you are well known, except God commanded you to be there like he commanded Isaac (Gen. 26:1-14). Most of those who know your background will never or have less regard for your product. The unfamiliar people who never know your background will inevitably unlock your best from you more.

Everybody will want to shine out the more in any place, where he or she is being applauded and celebrated, including you. But those that know you from your beginning may want to mute your effort because they may not believe in you. They will only begin to believe you when undeniable proofs begin to show out. **"A prophet is not honored in his own town,"** Jesus said.

**How to live a life void of fear of people**

1.  Know that life is a place of freedom, where everybody has the right to do what feels good to him or her (not stepping on the toes of others). So don't let anyone dominate your person unnecessarily.
2.  Know that you are in control over your life and not anyone else.
3.  Never mind what people say about your actions when it is a positive one. They are only displaying their dislike while it is your like.

4.  Live within the circle of life that is void of offence towards God and man. If your conscience is pure, never fear accusations.

If you can please God and yourself, you are at your best in life. Even when pleasing your spouse, let it not be against the will of God and his word. Perhaps people are pleased alongside, thank God; but if they are not, never try to please them, or else your life will be in confusion or go the wrong way (Luke 6: 26).

Know that what you enjoy doing is within your ability. If anyone is pleased with it, then you are sent to his or her way; but if not, know that he or she is not your beneficiary or your client.

7.  Avoid putting your hope in man. Make God your backbone and your final bus stop. Anyone you rely on will tend to exercise dominion over you unnecessarily. I have experienced it (see these Scriptures: Psalm 60: 11; 27:10).

**Let us continue with the enemies of success:**

4.  Slothfulness (Proverbs 10: 4; 12: 27; 22: 29; 19: 24; 18: 9; 24: 30-34; 13: 4): this is an attitude problem—not doing what is supposed to be done.
5.  Idleness: not willing to do anything about your vision. When ideas are not implemented, they become subject to decay (Ecclesiastes 10: 18).
6.  Procrastination (Ecclesiastes 11: 4): never look for a better or more convenient time to do your job when you can start from somewhere now.
7.  Discouragement (Joshua 1; 7, 8).
8.  Memory of past failures (Philippians 3: 12-14): stop mourning your past. Only correct your mistakes and keep going else, you miss the good things coming your way (Isaiah 43: 18, 19a).
9.  Allowing the opinion(s) of others to cloud over your God-given idea(s) (Proverbs 19: 27).
10. Distractions (Proverbs 4: 25-27).
11. Joy of past glory and achievement: always thinking you've arrived (Joshua 13: 1).

12. Traditions of men (general ways of doing things): learn to seek God's ways of doing what he asked you to do. 13. Never imitate people, except the Lord leads you to.

14. A wrong geographical location: every choice seed (vision) has a choice ground. Search it out with God. He will show you 'where'.

15. Wrong partnership (Proverbs 13: 20; 1 Corinthians 15: 33).

16. Comparison (2 Corinthians 10: 12).

17. Succumbing to oppositions.

18. Societal pressure: never listen to the ridicules of the society where you are. Statement like **"you are not fit for this"**, **"this is too local for you"**, or **"you can't afford this"**, etc. are what you must avoid if you must succeed in your pursuit.

I see God helping you! Everything holding you bound, I command them to break off from your life and destiny in the mighty name! Whatever has sunk your destiny among the above-mentioned enemies, I see God pulling you out of them all as you respond to his deliverance! You are free! Welcome to the mountaintop. Shine forth because your light has come! From this day, nothing will be able to stand against your journey to your destiny! You will fly high without boundaries in Jesus' precious name! Amen.

# CHAPTER TEN

## THE RULES OF SUCCESSFUL LIFE

A SUCCESSFUL LIFE IS a life well-spent in the will of God for you. It is God's kind of success. It is a life void of vain struggle(s). It is a life of excellence. It is also a life void of offence towards God and man and a life of fulfillment.

As I earlier said, success is not an accumulation of wealth, but it is the achievement of divine plan and purpose for your life; though wealth is necessary, and it is also God's will for you to prosper financially.

Why does God want you to have wealth? a. To satisfy your earthly needs towards the achievement of your divine goal (Philippians 4:19). b. To support God's work anywhere (2 Corinthians 9:8). c. To enable you provide for others (1Timothy 6:17-18). d. For your enjoyment (1 Timothy 6:17).

If you don't know those things above, you will be puffed up when God begins to prosper you financially.

# THE UNDENIABLE KEYS FOR SUCCESS IN LIFE

1. A well-defined purpose (1Corinthians 9:26): remember that when a revelation of God's plan for your life comes, you may tend to forget the full package. So, for this not to happen, do the following: a. Document your vision for a reminder (Habakkuk 2:2-3). b. Apply the law of autosuggestion. Think on your vision daily to allow better insight by divine illumination (Hebrews 2:1; Philippians 4:8; 2 Peter 1:19). c. Consult God daily for clarity (Psalm 119:130).

2. Concentration/focus (Proverbs 4:23-27): why should you guide your focus? a. It determines mastery over your pursuit. Holding on to a thing brings the best out of a man. b. It makes you concentrate your energy, money and time. c. It will seemingly bring your future closer to you in your mind. d. Broken focus creates instability, unending parade of prejudice, and unexpected tragedies in your life, according to Dr. Mike Murdock.

3. Information: having the knowledge of what you are to do to bring about the reality of your dream (Daniel 9:2; 1 Timothy 4:13, 15). How informed you are determines your shining in life.

Information makes you a potential star. Read more of this under the pursuit of information in chapter seven.

4. Planning (Proverbs 24:27): a. Know where life is taking you to b. device a plan to get there.

Planning means committing your thought to paper and mapping out possible strategies through which you can achieve your aim at view. It takes wisdom from above to really pursue a divine task (James 1:5; Proverbs 16:9; 24:3, 4; Luke 14:28-31).

Planning has no substitute. And remember, God will never plan for you but is ever ready to order your steps toward the achievement of your goal.

5.  Diligence: this is hard work, giving your vision all it takes in order to succeed (Proverbs 12:27; 14:23; 22:29; 12:11; 10:18; 21:25; 26; 21:17).

Why must you be diligent? a. To avoid starvation (Proverbs 19:15, 24). b. A working hand retains riches (Proverbs 13:11). c. It brings about accomplishment, which in return brings you joy at the end (Proverbs 13:12, 19). d. It will qualify you to sit among great people (Proverbs 22:29).

6.  Be willing to stand, when the wind of life blows. Learn to withstand oppositions when they come your way, and be persistent towards your heavenly calling— the purpose for your existence here on earth.

**Note:**

Life will certainly wage war with you, but I believe that the force of the vision ahead of you will definitely keep you moving.

7.  Have faith in God. Believe that God will bring his word to pass in your life (Romans 4:19-21).

8.  Fight the good fight of faith; lay hold on your vision. It must surely come to pass (1 Timothy 6:12; Habakkuk 2:3).

9.  Guide your life and vision with the governing laws of nature. (This will be discussed later in this chapter.)

10. Have a driving will to succeed. Never give up. Know that failure is always on the verge of success. So persist and see God leading you through (Luke 16:16). Don't join the bandwagon of failures.

**The notable pillars of success**

Success has five notable pillars among the above-mentioned keys on which man must stand; else, you are bound to fail. These notable pillars control and stand out among others, and they are as follows:

1.  A defined clear purpose
2.  Information
3.  Diligence (hard work)

4.  Character (good character model for living)
5.  Discipline (self-control or self management)

Also, be careful not to fall among these four categories of failures: a. Undecided b. Unfocused c. Unlearned d. Unexcited

**Diagram showing the notable pillars of success**

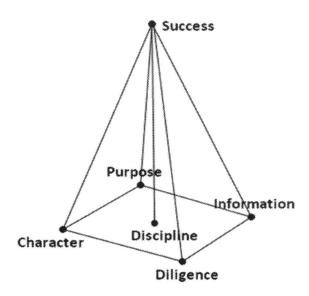

The control room for all is discipline. Until you are disciplined, you will never be able to keep yourself on the others. The Holy Spirit will help you in Jesus' name!

## THE BIBLICAL PRINCIPLES OF SUCCESS

*"This book of the law shall not depart out of thy mouth; but thou shalt meditate therein day and night, that thou mayest observe to do according to all that is written therein: for then thou shalt make thy way prosperous, and then thou shalt have good success"* (Joshua 1:8)

In this Kingdom of God, where we are, nothing works except its principle is known and systematically applied by divine guidance. Here are some of the biblical principles that make success a must:

1.  Be born again. Get alive in the Spirit. God is the God of the living, not of the dead. He can never relate to you the spiritual mysteries that pertain to your destiny until you come alive in the Spirit (John 3:3; 1 Corinthians 2:9-14). A natural man is living a life that is very parallel to that of God.

*"For God is Spirit, and those that must worship him must worship him in spirit and in truth"* (John 4:24)

Until you are having the same life with God, you can never understand his language when he speaks to you. You can never know your destiny until you are in touch with the Spirit of God, who relates spiritual matters to people as you read in 1 Corinthians 2:9-11; and you can never come in contact with God's Spirit until you are born again.

2.  Discover who you are, your purpose and how you are designed to function through divine insight (Ephesians 1:18; Ecclesiastes 6:9).
3.  Get in touch with the power of God to make you victorious over life's battles (Psalm 63:3; 1 John 5:4).
4.  Know your ability, and make use of it (Proverb 18:16; Proverb 17:8; Matthew 25:14-17).
5.  Be sensitive to God's signals concerning times, seasons and divine direction (Ecclesiastes 3:1-8, 11; 8:5, 6; 1 Chronicles 12:32; Psalm 32:8).
6.  Attend to the things you believe.
7.  Have no regard for the voice(s) of distractions (Nehemiah 4:1-3, 6; 2 Kings 2:1-6,13-15).
8.  Get connected to the Spirit of excellence (Daniel 6:3; Isaiah 32:15; 5:11, 12; Genesis 41:37-40; 41:44).
9.  Have confidence in God (Hebrews 10:35; 36; Numbers 14:1-9), or else, you will experience a breach of God's promise instead of its fulfillment (Numbers 14:34, 22-38). Never doubt God in whatever He tells you (1 John 5:10b).
10. Avoid the fear of people or death (Hebrews 2:15; Proverbs 29:25; Numbers 14:28-32; Job 3:25, 26).
11. Every opposition in life on your way to fulfilling your destiny always reminds you of your past mediocre life and makes it preferable in your eyes. Remember, it is the devil's trick; so don't

      look back (Luke 9:62; Numbers 13:32-33; 14:1-4; Exodus 14:10-12; Hebrews 10:38, 39).

12. Trust in the Lord, the fulfiller of dreams (Ezekiel 12:22-24; Jeremiah 29:11; Romans 4:17-21; Philippians 1:6; 1 Thessalonians 5:24; Hebrews 10:23).

13. let giving of praise and glory to God is your lifestyle (Zechariah 14:17, 18; Hebrews 3: 17-19; Malachi 2:1-3; Exodus 15:11; Psalm 67:5, 6; Deuteronomy 28:47, 48).

14. Carry, and stay in, God's presence always (Psalm 114:1-8; Deuteronomy 2:7; Acts 10:38; Exodus 33:13-17; John 3:1, 2; John 8:28, 29). Nothing makes a man achieve great exploits in the Lord like God's presence (Psalm 60:12; Luke 5:17; Acts 7:9, 10; 2 Samuel 6:11, 12; Isaiah 8:9, 10; 2 Samuel 5:10).

15. Never accept negative information or counsel contrary to what God wants you to do (Proverbs 19:27; 1:1-3).

16. If Lot must go with you, it is important you consult God first, or else, never let Lot go with you (Isaiah 51:1-3). Remember, until Lot left Abraham, God never showed him the Promised Land (Genesis 12:1-4; 13:14-18).

17. Seek counsel always from your mentors in your area of ignorance for adequate light, especially when in a fix and you know not what to do (Proverbs 20: 5; 11: 14; 15: 22; 20: 18; 24: 6).

18. Never settle in the circle of mediocrities; Climb to greater heights through mental and skill development on to perfection (2 Timothy 2: 15; Daniel 12: 3; 9: 2; 1Timothy 4: 13-16).

19. Be always attentive to God's Spirit daily (John 8: 26; 28, 29; 16: 13-15; 5:30).

20. Don't let the wrong person (Jonah), whose direction of life is different from yours, into your boat of life.

21. Communicate your worldly goods toward the spreading of God's Kingdom in order to promote and prosper the work of your hand (Luke 5: 1-7; 2 Corinthians 9: 8; Haggai 1: 4-10; Exodus 36: 1-7).

22. Pay and care for your workers well. Their success and well-being determine your success also (Proverbs 27:23-27).

23. Your tithe is your covenant trading capital or shares in God's hand. It is also your divine insurance. So don't eat it. It connects

you to your future. If you eat it, you are eating your financial future. It is your tax in God's kingdom, where you belong. If you withhold it, you will attract the wrath of heaven's government. Keep investing it in God's work. It is a hallowed covenant asset for increase (Malachi 3:8-12; 4:1, 2).

24. Learn to follow the wind of God's instruction daily in your life (Deuteronomy 32: 9-14; Isaiah 48: 17,18; 30: 21; Psalm 32: 8; 2 Samuel 2: 1, 2: 17-19, 22-25; Proverbs 16: 25).

25. Discipline yourself to speak (positively) in line with God's word concerning your life and endeavor always (Proverbs 6: 2; Matthew 12: 37; Numbers 14: 28; James 3: 5,6; Ecclesiastes 5: 6; Isaiah 44: 26; Job 6: 25).

26. Keep your joy ever living (Joel 1:12; Deuteronomy 28:47, 48; Habakkuk 3:17-19).

27. Please try by all possible means to stay focused on your vision always (Proverbs 4:25-27, Matthew 6:22; Luke 11:34).

28. Keep good and beneficial company only (Proverbs 13:20; Psalm 26:4; Proverbs 12:11; 28:19).

29. Make sure you marry the right person, and study about marriage properly in order to build your home. Remember, heaven is the administrative place for earthly endeavors. So, also, your home is the same to your assignment (Genesis 2:23, 24; Matt.19: 4-6).

30. Never despise the days of little beginnings (Zechariah 4:10; Job 8:7; Ezekiel 36:11; Ecclesiastes 7:8; Proverbs 4:18).

31. Be determined to succeed in life (1 Corinthians 9:24; Luke 16:16; 13:24). Remember the lepers at the gate of Samaria (2 Kings 7:3-8).

32. Avoid hastiness in life. Follow God phase by phase (Proverbs 28:20.22; Mark 4:26-29). God hates hastiness!

33. Be wise (Ecclesiastes 7:11, 12, 19; Proverbs 4:7).

34. Study the word of God daily, and keep them in your heart. Forget not to live by them (2 Peter 1:19; Hebrews 2:1; Joshua 1:8; Psalm 1:1-3; Isaiah 34:16).

35. Be diligent in your divine pursuit (Proverbs 14:23; 22:29; 24:30-34; 6:6-9; 12:27). Learn to rise up early from sleep.

36. Avoid sentiment in your life and endeavors. Your enemies could be the one you least or never expected, and they will definitely take

advantage of your sentimental lifestyle. So be sensitive (Matthew 10:36; Galatians 2:4-5; Psalm 55:12-14; 41:9; Nehemiah 4:11).

37. Discover the key to mastering adversity in life from these scriptures: 1 Peter 4:12-14; 2 Corinthians 4:16-18; 1 peter 5:10.

38. Live a liberal life toward humanity (Proverbs 11:24-26; 13:7; 21:3; 28:27; 22:9).

39. Learn to sow into the lives of men of God (Galatians 6:6; 1 Kings 17:8-24).

40. Honor your father and mother with your substances (Ephesians 6:2-3).

## SOME OF THE GOVERNING LAWS OF NATURE

I repeat, in this world everything has a law and this law is the platform on which desired result is born. Nothing happens on its own without your meeting its laid-down demand(s). You have your part to play to ensure the achievement of your desires, and you will get them before you leave this earth in Jesus' name! Please let's look at these laws together:

1. The law of destiny: this states that the life of a man depends on the purpose for which he is born, the right time for the execution of his assignment from his birth to his death, and the geographical location for the prosperity and success of his assignment (Luke 1:80). Until you discover your purpose and the place where God wants you to carry out the purpose, and be on time with God for every facet of your assignment, your life will never have any meaning.

2. The law of financial prosperity: this states that liberality is the soul of financial expansion, coupled with the destined work of your hand (Proverbs 11:25; 13:11; Luke 6:38).

3. The law of relationship: this states that relationship is the soul of success in life. There is no one-man island. You need somebody to succeed in life. You can never succeed alone. It also states that your inter-meddling will either make you or mar you (Proverbs 13:20; 1 Corinthians 15:30; Proverbs 27:17, 19). Relationships will definitely change you.

4. The law of the mind: this states that the quality of a man depends on the quality of his mentality; and that whatever enters the mind

as information through the eyes or ears has power to be transmuted into its physical counterpart or equivalence through the members of your body (Proverbs 4:23).

5.  The law of words: this states that every word a man speaks creates his circumstances. Words are seeds that produce their mates. They are used to carry what we see in the spirit Realm onto the physical realm. They are conveyors with which we convey the invisible to the visible (Hebrews 11:3; Romans 4:17), whether positive words or negative words.

6.  The law of devotion: this states that how much time you invest into your privacy for mental input (studying) or spiritual input (fellowship with God) determines your disposition and exploits in life: garbage in: garbage out (Matthew 7:1-21).

## What devotion does in the life of someone

When you observe devotion: a. You receive the latest that heaven wants to do. b. The conspiracy of the enemies is revealed to you. c. It makes you current with heaven's agenda. d. As rechargeable lantern, it charges us; and as the light of the world, we become a full light to our generation in the area of our calling. e. The more you devote, the more you shine from glory to glory (Proverbs 27:17, 19; 2 Corinthians 3:18). f. When we go in with God, our lapses are shown, our goals are corrected, our wounds are healed, our spiritual strength is renewed, and secrets are delivered into our hands. Remember Moses (Exodus 34) and Jesus (Mark 1:35; 6:46).

If you really want to keep going higher in life, never fail to abide by the law of devotion with God. It is the platform on which new ideas and strategies are birthed from God in order to know what to do and how to do it at a given time. Those who don't abide by the law of devotion lose color too soon. If you start very hot and well, and begin to reduce in terms of effectiveness, it is because of the neglect of the law of devotion.

God is the one who gave you the assignment. You therefore need to keep visiting God daily or as scheduled with him for consultation, revelation and impartation for greater exploit and higher attainment.

This will enable you to move from phase to phase and from glory to glory.

The altar of devotion is a place where you study God's word, have contact with the power of God, and receive divine instruction for breakthrough or for the next level.

Apostle Peter said, *"But we will give ourselves continually to prayer, and to the ministry of the word"* (Acts 6:4).

No wonder at a time in his life, his shadow healed the sick.

*"Insomuch that they brought forth the sick into the streets, and laid them on beds and couches, that at least the shadow of Peter passing by might overshadow some of them. There came also a multitude out of the cities round about unto Jerusalem, bringing sick folks, and them which were vexed with unclean spirits: and they were healed every one"* (Acts 5:15-16)

Devotion is it. This man Peter had been with Jesus. He had studied the ways of Christ, especially his devotional lifestyle. He witnessed him on Mount Sinai and saw what happened after he came down (Matthew 17:1-9, 14-21).

All the great men and women you are hearing of today are men of strong "devotion". If you can also abide by this law, you will go places in life.

Supernatural living is a product of endothermic reaction (staying in God's presence and absorbing divine life from Him). Examples: a. Electric bulb and power source. b. A cold iron placed in a hot fire does not remain the same, but rather it will be red hot. Jesus came out of the wilderness of prayer and fasting in the power of the Spirit, and His fame spread abroad (Luke 4:1-14). This is the product of devotion.

7.  The law of success: this states that an idea without a pursuit and without a constructive strategy to achieve it will never see the top of the mountain nor ride on the high places of the earth. Divine idea plus action plus divine wisdom equals divine success. If you believe in receiving divine ideas and following them up with

perspiration and wisdom from above you are not going to be far from a genius (Proverbs 12:27).

8.  The law of delegation: this states that if a man engages in a hundred men's work, he produces less or no result and dies before his time. Duplicate yourself into others, who can also help you, or employ capable hands that are also faithful (Exodus 18:14-18, 21-24; 2 Timothy 2:2).

9.  The law of Sabbath: this states that hard work without rest leads to early death (Exodus 31:16-18). Even God, who is a spirit, rested and was refreshed; so never overdrive yourself.

What about Jesus? There were times when he broke the traditional laws of men. He wouldn't round up in his crusades before he withdrew himself from the crowd in most cases (which is not normal for some present-day ministers) to go for rest with his disciples (Luke 6:30, 31).

One day, he was so occupied with programs that he became very tired and slept off when he was traveling on the sea. Thank God he was not the captain, otherwise, they would have crashed because he would have been dosing while driving the ship.

When you are bodily and mentally tired, there is a measure of anointing that you can't carry; certain measure will lift or diffuse from you, or else you may die. Your physical health and strength must be directly proportional to a certain measure of anointing before you are permitted to carry such anointing. If you have a mental fatigue, you will experience poor memory work, no matter how much load of knowledge you can carry in your brain. At this time, if you are not careful, the devil's strike can get you down because you can only fight the good fight of faith through the Scripture(s) you can remember (Ephesians 6:10-18). So learn to put your body and your brain to rest; else, you will wear out before your time.

When your body is weak, it will not be able to discharge what your spirit releases to it through your mind. And when your mind is fatigued, it will not be able to receive messages from your spirit. So learn to rest in order to be refreshed.

I put this to you also: if the demand on you in your business or ministry is becoming too much, mentor people and delegate work to them. Give less necessary work to them and major on the most necessary. Get yourself an assistant who can also handle what you can handle. Don't try to do all alone. You will live long in Jesus' name!

10.  The law of cause and effect: this states that whatever a man does, whether positive or negative, he must surely receive his reward (Ephesians 6:8; Galatians 6:9). Having known this, learn to do good to everyone that comes your way at all times (Matthew 7:12).

*"Blessed are the merciful, for they shall obtain mercy"* (Matthew 5:7)

Again, some people never like to do good things to those who do them evil. But instead of bearing grudges, which will definitely hinder your relationship with God or hinder your prayers from reaching heaven, why not show forgiveness and love? Jesus says, *"But I say unto you, Love your enemies, bless them that curse you, do good to them that hate you, and pray for them which despitefully use you, and persecute you"* (Matthew 5:44).

Read these Scriptures and see the advice of Paul the apostle for us all in God's Kingdom: Romans 12:9-14.

No matter what a man does to you, especially if it is evil, never relate back with evil, and God will surely fight for you. Believe what I am telling you because I also experience this always. Whatever you do will produce a harvest of its kind for you in the nearest future.

11.  The law of faith: this states that whatever a man believes works on his life and destiny (Matthew 8:13; 9:29).
12.  The law of dignity: this states that the character of a man and his relevance to his society and the world at large defines his worth (Proverbs 12:8).
13.  The law of the hidden man: this states that until a man talks or acts, nobody really knows him. And until a man reaches the climax of what he is really born to do, you can never really define who he is indeed. No container is defined by its design but by what it contains. So also is a man. The climax of your divine goal is equal

to the real you fully metamorphosed. Where your goal ends is where your life ends.

14. The law of leadership: this states that the quality of your humble service to the needs of humanity in the area of your endeavor determines the quantity of followers towards you. It will also determine the measure of influence you have on your generation. This makes you a leader in the first place. Greatness is being greatly responsible to the masses, your reward not missing.

15. The law of personal growth: this states that if you know more, act more on what you know, and delegate more to more people, you will grow more. So go for more information. It is the trade secret in the world of growth.

16. The law of miracles: this states that until one discovers or catches the understanding of covenant scriptural promises concerning an ugly situation, confesses it confidently, and acts upon its covenant demand(s), supernatural will not be experienced.

17. The law of repetition: this states that what you keep doing, you will soon master; what you keep hearing, you will soon understand, as soon as you capture a mental image of it; what you keep seeing, you will accept.

18. The law of reward: this states that if you look out for your reward in the hands of men, you may not get it; but make God your reward, and he will reward you through men's hands. It also states that if there is no service, there would no reward. Reward simply means a payment (of any kind) from God, through the instrumentality of man, for every service rendered.

Christianity is based upon the golden rule. You can find this golden rule in the following Scripture: Matthew 7:12. The number of problems you solve for humanity determines your measure of reward in life from God, through men's hands.

Any position you occupy in life is all about relevance and responsibility. Every man is born to solve a particular problem for his generation and the world at large. Therefore, it is very important in life for you to be problem-solving conscious. One gift in your hand is worth millions of rewards in life, depending on the measure of its utility to the benefit of mankind.

**How to connect yourself to the reward(s) of heaven**

1.  Do what God asked you to do in life (Deuteronomy 28:1, 2; Psalm 32:8; Isaiah 48:17, 18)

2.  Have a merciful heart towards others (Matthew 5:7; Isaiah. 58:7-14; Proverbs 11:24-26; 21:13; Psalm 41:1-3)

3.  Commit yourself to the promotion of God's Kingdom (Matthew 6:33)

4.  Labor with your hands based on your purpose and calling in life to affect your generation and the world at large (Proverbs 14:23)

19. The law of time: this states that your respect for or attitude towards time determines the success or failure of your business and finance. If you cannot respect your personal time, you can't respect the time of others also. Time is made for profitable investment and not for wastage.

20. The law of attitude: this states that your attitude determines your altitude in life, both in relationship and business; so develop your character to enhance your interpersonal skill, a booster to your endeavor. Have a positive attitude towards life and people.

21. The law of self development: this states that until you acquire more information based on life and your purpose for existing, you are bound to be limited in life, and you may end up being a mediocre or a local champion in your small vicinity. You cannot see beyond the level of positive information you have acquired into your mind concerning life (Ecclesiastes 2:14).

22. The law of focus: this states that what you keep seeing or doing determines your direction and success. Focus determines mastery.

23. The law of personal fulfillment: this states that fulfillment is not in the accumulation of wealth but in daily achievement of your divine purpose from phase to phase until the metamorphosis of your destiny is completed.

24. The law of divine geography: this states that for the success of your destiny to be established or accomplished, the geographical locations meant for it per time (from your birth to death) must be attended.

There are several people who attended the School of Geography before reaching the peak of their destinies. These individuals are as follow:

1.  Abraham: he moved to Canaan, where God prospered him (Genesis 12:1-5).
2.  Isaac: he found his wife in his mother's place among her kindred. He also prospered in Philistine (Genesis 26:1-14).
3.  Jacob: he located his wives and began to enjoy prosperity in Laban's community (Haran).
4.  Joseph: he, by slavery, entered Egypt (outside of his country) where everything, including his marriage and lifting, according to his dream, happened.
5.  Moses: he was born in the land of bondage (Egypt), grew there, located his purpose for existing beside a mountain in Midia (in the burning bush), where he also found his destined wife given to him by favor (Exodus 2:11-22; 3: 1-10).
6.  Jephthah: he fled from his brethren to the land of Tob, where he discovered his talent as a warlord, trained fighters and made his way to the top as a king among the same brethren who before this time had chased him away (Judges 11: 12-7).
7.  Ruth: she left Moab, her own place, with her mother-in-law for Bethlehem, her mother-in-law's place, where she found her new, destined husband called Boaz (Ruth 1: 15-22; 2, 3, 4).
8.  Elijah: he ran to Zarephath by God's instruction, where he located survival from famine caused by drought (1Kings 17: 1-16).
9.  Ezra: he was born in the land of exile called Persia, where he located the favor of financial and material sponsorship for God's assignment in his life (Ezra 7: 1-28).
10. King Saul: when he was looking for his father's ass, he changed location and eventually located his kingship destiny in the hand of Samuel, the prophet of God (1 Samuel 9:10).
11. Nehemiah: captivity had to happen in order for him to locate himself in a place, where he discovered his purpose: rebuilding of Jerusalem's wall and gates (Nehemiah 1:1-11; 2:1-18). In that same place, he located divine provision that made his divine assignment possible.
12. Esther: she found her destiny by locating her destined husband, not in Israel but in the land of captivity (provinces of one hundred

and twenty seven, from India to Ethiopia). Her husband was the king of these provinces (Esther 2: 5-17). Isn't that great?

13. Daniel: he was the top President who governed along side with Shadrach, Meshach and Abednego in the land of Babylon, not in their native land, Israel (Daniel 2: 48, 49). You will locate yours in Jesus' name!

14. John: he began his purpose in the wilderness, according to prophecy (Luke 3: 1-4).

15. Jesus: he had a place to be born, and a place to die according to prophecy (Luke 2: 1-19).

May the law of geography play its perfect role in your life to help you fulfill your destiny in Jesus' name!

Let's continue with the governing laws of nature:

25. The law of Justice: this states that God will make happen to you what you make happen to others (Luke 6: 37, 38; Ephesians 6:8; Matthew 7:12).

26. The law of mercy: this states that the only true key to the door of mercy is liberality and showing of mercy to others (Luke 6:27-34; Proverbs 11: 25; Matthew 5: 7; Proverbs 21: 13).

As you apply yourself to work with and walk in these governing laws of nature discovered, I see you flying high without hindrances in Jesus' name!

# CHAPTER ELEVEN

## THE POWER OF DIVINE DIRECTION

THE SUCCESS OF EVERY divine vision is impossible without divine direction. Divine direction is not by human mental calculation. Divine success does not answer to human struggle. No man knows the way to the top of life except God. There is only one person who leads the way, and that person is Jesus. He says, *"I am the way, the truth, and the life . . ."* (John 14:6).

If God gives vision, then God himself must direct it. God is your employer, and you are his employee. You can never dictate for God nor do it your own way; neither in your own time nor just the place you feel. God does. He is the head of the Kingdom. Instruction comes from him. You cannot go against his authority and go away with it.

Why many fail while running with God's vision is because they don't have a place of contact with heaven, where God will give directive(s) concerning their pursuit(s) on a round table. Nothing excites God like your being a man after his own heart; nothing grieves him like running his vision your own way.

To God's mandate delivered onto a man, there is a divine plan, a set time and a place for it. So, not consulting the mind of God is to ignore your director. If you don't take your time, you are bound to lose your job in God's company.

God gave Moses an instruction to bring the children of Israel out of Egypt; he also gave him instructions on what to do to Pharaoh and the Egyptians. Not only that, from time to time Moses kept asking him on what to do whenever he was faced with situations, or was confused on the way, or whenever any given instruction was achieved and there was nothing to do to go forward. All these were geared toward the success of the mandate given to him.

## FOLLOWING GOD TO THE TOP OF LIFE

Let us talk about a man who was after the heartbeat of God in his time:

**David:** this was a man, who believed in a round-table talk with God. When I talk about a round-table talk, I mean the application of the law of devotion with God. God is always ahead of us when he gives us an assignment. He is always involved in every work he puts into the hands of men that he trusts. He sees well than we see.

In Isaiah 55:8, 9, He said, *"For my thoughts are not your thoughts, neither are your ways my ways, said the Lord. For as the heavens are higher than the earth, so are my ways higher than your ways, and my thoughts than your thoughts."*

The bible also says that his ways are past finding out. That is, you cannot search them out, except he shows them to you. The Bible says, *"He made known his ways unto Moses, his acts unto the children of Israel"* (Psalm 103:7).

The Psalmist also made this statement: *"The Lord is my shepherd, I shall not want"* (Psalm 23:1).

He is also known as Jehovah Roi—the Lord our Great Shepherd. Peter the Apostle called Jesus the Chief Shepherd.

## Prerequisites for divine direction

There are certain qualifications you need to possess before you will be entitled to God's leading. These qualities are as follows:

1.  Accepting your human limitation: the bible says, *"Trust in the Lord with all your heart, and lean not to your own understanding"* (Proverbs 3:5). It also says, *"Be not wise in thine own eyes . . ."* (Proverbs 3:7).

Most times when you make plans, you still see them happening in the way you never thought of because, you did not allow God to guide you.

*A man's heart deviseth his way but the Lord directeth his steps"* (Proverbs 16:9)

2.  Trust in the Lord for his leading

*"Commit thy way unto the Lord; trust also in him; and he shall bring it to pass"* (Psalm 37:5)

3.  Possessing a meek heart

*"The meek will he guide in judgment: and the meek will he teach his way"* (Psalm 25:9)

God never leads a proud man. A proud man is full of himself. Moses was termed the meekest man on earth in his time. No wonder God led him all through because, he acknowledged his imperfection.

*". . . God resisteth the proud but giveth grace unto the humble"* (James 4:6)

*"Submit yourself unto God . . ."* (James 4:7)

4.  Fearing God

*"What man is he that feareth the Lord? Him shall he teach in the way that he shall choose"* (Psalm 25:12)

If you are someone that fears God, you will always seek his will or his mind for every step you take in life as you journey toward your success or the top of life. Why did God reject Saul, the king of Israel? It is because he is a man that did things in his own way, and not after the mind of God. And God said, **"He has ceased from following me."** He feared people more than God (1 Samuel 15:10, 11, 24).

What is our confidence that God will always be willing to lead us in the way to the top of life? God says, *"I will instruct thee and teach thee in the way which thou shalt go: I will guide thee with mine eye"* (Psalm 32:8).

David knew this! That was why he kept consulting God throughout his life time (2 Samuel 2:1-3; 5:17-25; 1 Samuel 23:1-14).

David never believed in assumption nor was he sentimental in life. That he helped the people of Keilah never made him think that they would not deliver him into the hands of King Saul; neither did he go to consult them for help. He never trusted any one more than God.

That he defeated the Philistines the first time never made him go against them again with the mind of the first strategy. But he consulted the mind of God on the matter. He believed solely in the counsel of God. No wonder God called him a man after his own heart. He believed that whenever God said go, he would surely be with him.

Look at his statement in these Scriptures: 2 Samuel 22:30-51. He made God his confidence. How would God not help him?

So, if you really want to reach the high place in life, you better learn how to follow God through his daily instructions. How do you do this? You do this by hearing his voice through your spirit man. God will always speak to his sons and daughters (Psalm 32:8, 9).

The word of God says, *"And thine ears shall hear a word behind thee, saying, this is the way, walk ye in it, when ye turn to the right hand, and when ye turn to the left"* (Isaiah 30:21).

# THE EVIDENCES OF DIVINE DIRECTION

Someone may ask, "How shall I know when God is leading me?" To give you the assurance of his leading, here are the evidences thereof:

1.  He leads in the way of peace. There will be great peace in your heart when you hear from God (Isaiah 48:17, 18)
2.  God's awesome presence will always be with you, and you will definitely know it (Acts 10:38, Luke 5:17)
3.  Because his presence is with you, prosperity will be evident in the work of your hands (Deuteronomy 2:7; Gen. 26:1-14)
4.  When God leads you, he will make sure you have provision for living (1 Kings 17:1-16). I have always enjoyed this.
5.  When God leads you, everywhere you go, you will always experience people's acceptance and favor (Luke 9:51-53)
6.  God's divine protection will make a hedge around your life and pursuit (Genesis 31:11-29; Exodus 14:9-20; Numbers 22:23; Isaiah 63:9)
7.  Your heart will always be full of joy, and you will live in divine pleasure (Psalm 16:11)
8.  You will always have a sweatless success (Deuteronomy 23:19-14)
9.  The last one I will mention here is that God will always impart faith in you to enable you to accomplish your divine goal courageously and confidently (Joshua 1:1,6,7)

Jesus is the author and finisher of our faith. He imparts it and He helps us to use it to the end for profitable result (Hebrews 12:2a). Every instruction God gives you he will surely impart into you the equivalent faith for accomplishment.

Faith and divine wisdom are synonymous. They come the same way and they walk hand in hand. God will never give you instruction without imparting into you these two instruments for divine achievement.

Faith is a divine proof that gives you an assurance that your goal will be achieved, while wisdom gives you direction and understanding to enable you to know when and how to go about your vision.

Faith offers confidence and boldness for achievement, while wisdom offers excellence in your achievement. Faith offers courage to climb the mountains, while wisdom teaches you the way to follow to the top (Hebrews 11:1; Ecclesiastes 10:10). Faith births in you a divine zeal, but wisdom helps you to be discreet in your affairs.

All these appear in your life when you are under a divine leading. Faith and divine wisdom do not work when you are pursuing ambition because God fights against human ambitions.

*"The Lord brings the counsel of the nations to nothing; He makes the plans of the people of no effect"* (Psalm 33:10)

Supernatural faith and divine wisdom are not given by God for your human ambition or for pleasure (just to brag with them), but they are given as divine instruments for the accurate achievement of the seemingly 'impossible', when pursuing a divine instruction. Until you come in contact with God's mandate for your life, you will never experience these things I am really talking about, and you will never experience all those benefits mentioned above.

## How does God lead?

The major thing that will make you understand and really follow God to the end is having a spiritual sensitive antenna that catches up with the wave of God's frequencies in the realm of the spirit.

Let's talk about the way God leads:

1.  He leads you by his word (logos) as you read the bible.
2.  He leads you by speaking to your spirit (rhema).
3.  He leads you by giving you revelation, either through dreams or trances (Job 33:14-18; Numbers 24:16). Remember, God speaks in pictures!

You can never be surer of your steps when men tell you what God is saying than when God speaks to you personally.

**How can you hear God's voice?**

1.  By being sensitive to him every day of your life
2.  By reading his word daily for daily guidance
3.  By listening to the Holy Spirit in your spirit
4.  By being attentive to the revelations God shows to you every day of your life
5.  By being upon your watch (meditation) (Habakkuk 2:1-2)

God will always speak; just be willing to listen!

# CHAPTER TWELVE

## CRAVING FOR EXCELLENCE IN LIFE

"EXCELLENCE", ACCORDING TO ADVANCED Learner's Dictionary, means "the quality of being extremely good or outstanding." That is, standing out among the crowd.

Every believer is born by an excellent God. Also the spirit of excellence rests upon every true believer, but it is your responsibility to explore the Kingdom's covenant secrets that make for excellence in a man's endeavor and life.

The Bible says, *"And they that be wise shall be as the brightness of the firmament . . ."* (Daniel 12: 3a).

*"A man's wisdom maketh his face to shine . . ."* (Ecclesiastes 8: 1b)

*"The wise shall inherit glory: but shame shall be the promotion of fools"* (Proverbs 3: 35)

Nothing makes a man's life and work to be excellent like the wisdom of God. Remember Solomon!

To shine or to inherit glory means to live an excellent life. You can never live an excellent life without first of all coming in contact with the spirit of excellence.

To be outstanding in life means to be above others within the sphere of your kind of calling. It also means doing everything well without stepping on the toes of others or without having an offence toward God or man, and doing everything to the glory of God.

Every man's work is the output of his summation, or the portrait of what he contains, either foolishness or wisdom.

Remember, the bible says, *"I wisdom dwell with prudence, and find out knowledge of witty inventions. By me kings reign, and princes decree justice"* (Proverbs 8: 12, 15).

You can never have this kind of wisdom and not be creative or innovative in life. This ability to be creative or innovative will always put you ahead of common men, and also will surely make you outstanding in life just as it did for Joseph. Read his account in the following passages of the bible (Genesis 41: 1-44, 47-49).

You can't have this wisdom of God and not be in dominion, no matter your age. Joseph was just thirty years when he became a ruler in Egypt, and was next to Pharaoh. Read the following passages of the bible and discover the exploits of divine wisdom (Proverbs 8: 12-36).

I see you having the dividends of divine wisdom in your life in Jesus' name!

See that you never give an excuse with your age. Jesus was twelve, when he began to question and answer questions concerning the things of God. The bible says, *"Great men are not always wise: neither do the aged understand judgment"* (Job. 32: 9).

It is the inspiration of God that gives people understanding. The bible says, *"But there is a spirit in man: and the inspiration of the Almighty giveth him understanding"* (Job. 32: 8).

This inspiration is the product of the Holy Ghost Himself (2 Timothy 3:16a; 2 Peter 1: 21). According to Bishop David O. Oyedepo, **"Inspiration is defined as the movement of the Spirit of God on your mental region."** Application of ideas from God is wisdom.

All the patriarchs of the bible time, who were excellent, were men that feared God. They were always looking for the mind of God in all things before taking steps, just like David the king (2 Samuel 4: 1-4; 23: 1-14).

## The necessary steps to the peak of excellence

1. Be filled with the Holy Ghost. When you are filled with the Spirit of God, ideas about your destiny will be unfolded to you (Luke 4:18, 19). Wonderful result is what you will see in your endeavor (Mark 6:2), and the following will be upon your life—the seven 'Spirits' of God:

1. The Spirit of the Lord
2. The Spirit of wisdom
3. The Spirit of understanding
4. The Spirit of counsel
5. The Spirit of might
6. The Spirit of knowledge
7. And the Spirit of the fear of the Lord (Isaiah 11:2)

These benefits of God's Spirit are grouped into two parts:

1. Wisdom
2. Power

Knowledge, understanding, counsels, wisdom and the fear of the Lord are under **"wisdom"**, while might and the Spirit of the Lord are under **"Power"**.

Whenever the Spirit of the Lord comes upon you, he anoints you and empowers you to do certain things for God and for men (Luke 4:18; Romans 15:19; Acts 1:8).

Until God anoints you for your divine mandate, you will never go far in life. The anointing of God makes life colorful. It makes a difference between a failure and a success. If we pretend not to be in need of it, we will regret when we see the gap between us and those who have the anointing—the power of God to do extra-ordinary things in this ordinary world.

**Why must we go for the anointing?**

1.  It makes for an explosion in your pursuit or the work of your hands (Luke 4:1-14). The anointing also brought the disciples to limelight, after the baptism in the Holy Ghost, and wonders began to happen in their ministries (read the book of Acts of the Apostles).

2.  It gives you the power of revelations and divine insight into life's issues—knowing the "what" and "how" of things (not working in the dark nor being confused), and making you avoid assumptions—trial-and-error kind of life (1 John 2:27; 1 Corinthians 2:9-12).

3.  It makes you be relevant to your environment and the social world as it begins to help you solve problems around where you are or anywhere you go (Acts 10:38; Mark 1:32-34). Remember the patriarchs.

4.  It makes you be easily recognized in your society (Genesis 41:1-14; Daniel 5:1-12; Acts 10:1-6; 9:36-41; 5:14-16).

You shall be announced by the anointing as you receive it in Jesus' name!

To make excellence our watch-word,

1.  Follow God's directions by taking heed to his instructions daily (Isaiah 30:21; Psalm. 32:8; Deuteronomy 28:1, 2)

2.  Always ask for his wisdom in everything you do in life to ensure excellent results (James 1:5)

3.  Maintain wise relationships and be in the company of godly, positive people (Proverbs 13:20; Daniel 2:17, 47-49). Daniel never intermeddled with ungodly people at all. No wonder he made excellence a watchword in his life. Praise God! Hallelujah!

4.  Be a reader of positive books, mostly in the area of your calling and purpose in life (Daniel 9:2; 1 Timothy 4:13, 15-16).

5.  Go for both formal and informal education—seminars, conferences, tapes of great men and women, people's biographies, etc. Attend an institution based on your vision. Never fail to learn how to travel to places you have never been before. It will make you to meet with new ideas and people with great insight, who would also inspire you. What you see affects your thought, and

your thought must surely affect your vision. This will deliver you from the valley of mediocrities in life (Proverbs 4:23; Galatians 4:1, 2).

6.  Talking about Jesus, he sat under tutors to enable him to go far in his ministry. So, why not you follow His steps?

7.  Learn to meditate, and don't fail to put down your inspirations or ideas gotten in black and white. A man once said, **"A shortest pencil is better than the longest memory."** If I had not been writing mine down, I would have not been able to write this book, when the time came, as a born author. It never took me any difficulty to write this book.

8.  Have a positive mental attitude toward life or proper positive mindset for right living (Proverbs 23:7).

9.  Seek the ideas and knowledge of true mentors just as Timothy sought after the knowledge of Paul the Apostle (Malachi 2:7; Proverbs 15:22).

10. Maintain focus on your calling and vision (Proverbs 4:24-27; 1 Corinthians 7:24).

11. Learn to listen to the Holy Spirit by being a thinker (Acts 10:19).

12. Ensure you remain in the presence of God always (Psalm 92:10-12).

13. Have a medical, financial and legal adviser around you in order to know how to manage your body, finance and legal issues that confront you in life. They will help you organize your steps well (not undermining the leading of God also).

14. Learn to wake up early and never be slothful in writing down your inspiration received during early morning meditations (Songs of Solomon 5:17, 22; Isaiah 50:4, 5; Proverbs 8:34, 34).

15. Make good use of your night seasons (Psalm 16:7; 19:2). Learn to meditate in the night. The atmosphere is always quiet. So, you can easily be inspired at that time. Many great people who lived before us did this.

You will excel!

# CONCLUSION

THIS WORLD IS A place of potential display. You are a seed of destiny planted here to germinate, grow and yield your fruits for the world at large to benefit from. Your ability to scale through huddles of life, walk wisely with God and men, explore the benefits of your greatest asset (the mind) understand the rules of success, study to make yourself approved, a workman that needs not to be ashamed, follow the governing laws of nature, and lots more, just as this book has taught you, will surely determine your success in the pursuit of your divinely discovered assignment.

Remember, destiny never fails on its own except you fail it yourself. Its success relies on the discovery of purpose for existing, following divine program from phase to phase, and locating the right places for its fulfillment.

Never forget, your faith is important. If it dies on the way, your failure is inevitable. So keep believing your vision and the God that showed it to you. It will surely come to pass.

Never fail to follow God's instructions daily from time to time. The Lord is with you. You will surely make it.

See you at the top!

# WORD FOR THOUGHT

TRUE SUCCESS IS IMPOSSIBLE without God! No man can really make true success without Jehovah Almighty, from whom all blessings flow, and whose blessings add no sorrow to the beneficiaries thereof (Proverbs 10:22; James 1:17).

It will be good for you, if you are not in Christ, to come into Christ, by whom your fruitfulness is possible (John 15:4, 5). It is evident that the way of the transgressor is hard (Proverbs 13:15). Take a look at these Scriptures: Job 15:20-30,34; 11:20; 18:5-21; 20:4-29; 27:11-23; 22:21-29; 36:8-12; Proverbs 28:9,13.

Therefore, if you are convinced, and you want to give your life to Christ, say this prayer after me:

**Lord Jesus, have mercy on me. Forgive me my sins. Wash my sins away with your precious blood. Cancel my name from the book of death and hell. Write my name in the book of life. Deliver me completely from sin, death and Satan. Come into me and stay. I accept you as my Lord and personal Savior. Thank you, Jesus, for saving me. Amen.**

So now that you are saved, I like you to go to a Church that teaches the truth, get baptized in water and in the Holy Ghost with the evidence of speaking in tongues as you are now fully welcome into the body of our Lord and Savior, Jesus Christ. God bless you!

I see every chain of the enemy around you and holding you in captivity shattering away in the name of Jesus! You are free today!

You are welcome to your world of undeniable and inevitable success. Keep succeeding till Christ comes or until your time here on earth is over in the glorious name of Jesus Christ! Hallelujah!

# About the Author

Prophet Harrison I. Enudi is the President of Destiny Awareness Outreach (A non-denominational ministry). He is a teacher of God's word, and an author with over 14,000 readers on Scribd.com. His life and ministry has really been a blessing and an inspiration to many people around the world, especially in United State, African and Asian continent.

His ministry borders around the teaching of 'Destiny', 'Success', 'Marriage', and 'The Supernatural'. As a Prophet, he also operate in the prophetic with healing and deliverance anointing. He is a man being sort for in regards to seminars, conferences and various churches. He graduated from Portable Bible School located in Kaduna, Nigeria; and also, from Word of Faith Bible Institute, Lagos, Nigeria.

Prophet Harrison is a divine instrument for bringing a transformation in the lives of people, healing to the sick, revival to the body of Christ, bringing people into their destinies, and for helping the children of God to discover their full spiritual ability and capacity in Christ, in order to help them keep the devil under their control, be in charge of their destinies, spiritual environment, and all forms of situation that emerges around their lives. He is this end-time divine instrument for the raising of champions and spiritual leaders in Christ.

Also, he is the author of two life-changing books titled, "Expressing the supernatural". The book was published is the United States of America, and it is being marketed worldwide, especially through the biggest bookstores—Amazon.com, borders.com, and barnesandnoble.com.

Please, you can visit his website at www.pastorharrisonenudi.org.